the modern
Chakra
guide

7 Steps to Awakening Your Energy in Today's World

By

CAROL TUTTLE

Dressing Your Truth®, Energy Profiling®, and Energy Type℠
are trademarks or registered trademarks of
Carol Tuttle Enterprises, LLC.

Library of Congress Control Number: 2019913266
ISBN: 978-0-9844021-5-1

Cover design by Timothy Kavmark
Text layout by TeaBerry Creative

Live Your Truth Press
support@liveyourtruth.com
liveyourtruth.com
Draper, Utah

Table of Contents

Part One

• • • • • • •

"Healing is awakening.
As we heal, we awaken to the
truth that God created us as
we are. As we *become* our true
selves, we get to learn how to act
on this newfound knowledge.
Every day we get that chance."

—CAROL TUTTLE

Stepping Onto the Path of Awakening

• • • • • • •

I found the chakras because I was desperate. I was 30 years old, a young mother of four children under the age of six, and my life was secretly falling apart. I wasn't looking for the metaphysical; I was just looking to get through the day. But when the study of chakra energy found me, it woke me up to a bright, fulfilling life that I couldn't have imagined when I was in that dark place.

If I could pass along a message about that journey of awakening, it would be this: There is more waiting for you. You just have to step into it.

Whether you feel as desperate as I did, or your life is going great, or you have a nagging sense that life as it is doesn't satisfy, it's time for you to awaken to a new energy that transforms you for the better. That is what this book will help you do—and now is the best time you could do it.

We live in a time when newly activated energies are changing the way we experience ourselves, each other, and the world. You're feeling this shift and seeing its effects play out, whether you realize it or not. Today's world can seem like a lot of commotion, confusion, and fear, especially if you're not aware of what is happening energetically. We are in a transition between an old energy and a new energy that affects our human experience, and if you understand that transition, you can move through it with more balance and ease. The old energy was the norm for the human experience for generations. The new energy is an opportunity for us to create a new experience, both individually and as a group. My chakra teachings address this modern-day shift, so that you can step into an even better life than you could have ever imagined.

The energy of the planet is shifting. We can compare our energy system to a computer program being upgraded to 2.0. We do not have a conscious choice if we want the upgrade. The fact that we are here, in our bodies, tells me that our souls already chose it for us. When this upgrade or new energy is unconscious to you, it can cause havoc and chaos in your life. It can put things into a tailspin, shift relationship dynamics, affect your professional life, and have a huge impact on your body if you don't know what's happening and how to work with it. This book will teach you the seven energy centers—the chakras—and how to consciously work with them as you move through this energetic shift. I will help you understand both the old and new energy in more depth in this book. All you need to know for now is that the transition from old to new energy is happening, whether you choose it or not. Your choice is how to navigate the change. By becoming a conscious manager of your personal energy system, you will tap into your own personal power and prevent the transition from ruling your life. This book will provide you with practical, easy-to-understand principles, and easy-to-use techniques that will get you working with your chakra energy right away, and will prove helpful, whether you're a new or advanced chakra student.

Part One of this book will help you see how your chakra energy system affects you as a whole, in our present day. I will not share the ancient teachings of the chakra energy system, but rather the new understanding I have received about these powerful energies, and how they are affecting you in today's world.

Part Two will guide you through each chakra in depth, particularly that chakra's modern manifestation. You may be surprised at how certain frustrations, challenges, or experiences are really just signs of the new energy available to us all. By awakening to this new energy and experiencing it consciously, you will upgrade your life.

If you've read other books on chakras, you'll know that many of those books speak in general terms about chakra order, color, and function. Some of that information will also be included here, and you will be able to refer back to it easily. But in this book, I will also share some highly personal experiences to illustrate what it can look like for the chakra energies to manifest and activate in your life. I want to help you see, in practical terms, how challenges in your life can be healed and transformed by working with your chakra energy. Individual stories are one of the best ways to learn, remember, and awaken.

So that's where we'll begin—with a story.

. . . .

In my 30's, I was a classic "superwoman," pushing hard to be the type of woman I thought I had to be. While staying home with four small children, I also ran a small business, served as PTA president, served in many of my church's service roles, planted beautiful flowers, grew a summer garden, cooked gourmet meals, sewed clothing for my children, and *always* kept a clean house. I became a perfectionist—someone who would take on too much and was always very busy. By all appearances I looked nearly perfect. I heard frequently how well I did everything. I was the envy of others because of my accomplishments.

That was my public side.

My private side was very different. Due to the lack of parental guidance and support I experienced in my childhood and teens, I gravitated toward becoming a very religious person for guidance and direction in my life. I also had extremely low self-esteem and found that strict obedience to what I believed was right became my crutch to help me feel better about myself. I lived my life in accordance with a belief that I was bad, and that bad people have to do a lot of good things to make up the difference. Through the years, I started to decline mentally and emotionally. I struggled with eating disorders, bouts of low self-esteem, depression, and other challenges. All those things had seemed like ordinary obstacles that I could overcome, but after the birth of my fourth child, I hit an all-time emotional low. I went from a dysfunctional life to a non-functional one, where suicidal depression was the mood of the day. Anger seeped in and rage burst out at inappropriate times, hurting me and my family on a regular basis. Trying to meet the needs of my family seemed overwhelming. I had days when I could barely get out of bed and see the day through, but nobody on the outside knew it. I got to the point where I no longer wanted to go on living because life was too painful. I had never felt such darkness, despair, and confusion. I knew I couldn't keep this up, so I enrolled myself in talk therapy with a psychologist.

Powerful rage often got the best of me. It seemed to come from nowhere and fill my whole body. One afternoon, I found my toddler son drawing on a wall with magic markers. I went crazy. I knew enough not to hurt him but I felt as if I could. I took myself into the other room and broke a chair, screaming and agonizing at the same time. My children fled from me. An unpredictable, raging mother of four small children is not a pretty sight, but it was my reality. I called my husband at work, pleading for him to come home. He came home immediately because he knew I was not safe alone with the children. We were all scared and I felt very, very guilty as I sat and wept. Jon insisted that I call my counselor, which I did, and he was able to see me that day.

In his office, my psychologist told me that I needed immediate help. Here I was, a mother at home alone from fourteen to sixteen hours a day with an infant, a two-, a three-, and a six-year-old. My therapist helped me understand that my confining circumstances tapped into my core feelings of powerlessness and fear. To counteract these feelings I'd go into an uncontrollable rage. He insisted I hire in-home help to prevent future out-of-control episodes and the risk of hurting my children. He told me that if I did not get immediate help he would have to admit me to the hospital as a psychiatric patient.

This was difficult for me to accept. Thoughts raced through my head: "I'm a do-it-all, do-it-well, superwoman. Women in my church don't hire outside help. What would people think? What about the money?"

The idea of going to the psych ward—when no one outside of my husband and children even knew I was struggling with inner demons—was not an option for me. So I hired a nanny, prayed harder, studied more, did as much right as I could, only to still want to end my life day after day.

What was wrong? Was it me? Was I unworthy? Did I not do enough? I had gripped the belief that obedience = happiness so tightly. If that formula were true, I should be the happiest person on the planet. But I was destroying my children, my marriage was hanging by a thread, and I was miserable. More than that, I felt angry that the formula was not working for me.

My therapist had told me I would always need to be in therapy to manage my issues. That sounded like stabilizing recovery, but not actual healing. Somewhere in me, I had a vision of finding true healing and happiness. So I prayed. I prayed honestly and let God know how angry I was. I told God, "I want to heal. I'm not settling for this. I will do whatever it takes, but show me what to do. Point me in the right direction."

I wasn't prepared for the answer that came in the form of a kind, unassuming woman who was old enough to be my mother. She actually lived up the street from me and went to the same church that I did. We hadn't spoken much before, but I suddenly felt the urge to seek her out and when I did, she adopted me as her daughter in healing. Her name was Betty and she was there to hold my hand through some of the hardest years of my life.

Betty introduced me to the world of energy healing and invited me to learn about the power and role of a human being's personal energy system. I didn't know much about it. In fact, I resisted the idea of studying energy healing at first. Questions came to mind: Who does this sort of thing? What will people think? Is it okay? Is energy healing compliant with my religious beliefs?

Desperation and pain are interesting teachers. I was a mom in a suburban neighborhood, trying to look perfect, but on the inside, I was living in a PTSD hellhole, wanting to kill myself. Because I was still in so much emotional pain after 2½ years of therapy, I felt more open to alternatives than I might have otherwise. I wasn't seeking out the metaphysical for the fun of it. I honestly believe it was brought into my life because I was so earnest in my prayers to find my way. One day, after a very difficult morning, my feelings of worthlessness washed over me more powerfully than I had ever before felt them. I still remember that day vividly. I dropped to my knees and sobbed as I realized how really bad I felt inside: worthless, powerless, and very, very vulnerable. The answer God gave me was to study what is now known as energy healing or energy medicine.

So I took the step. I stepped on that path, not knowing that I was about to learn about and activate seven of the most powerful energy centers that make up the mainframe of our personal energy system—the chakra energies. Little did I know where it would take me, or that I would be awakened to a truth about myself that I had no idea even existed.

I stepped on my path of awakening in 1991, when I made the choice to learn about the chakra energy system. I committed to a 9-month training program that met in person weekly, along with home study assignments and practicum hours. People who haven't studied energy healing personally sometimes imagine that this work involves strange or mysterious activities. But in our weekly trainings, there were no seances, no burning incense, no chanting, no religious teachings to study, and no worship services to attend. Instead, I studied with a notebook, training from my instructor, and practices to participate in. The focus of this 9-month training was to learn about the seven chakra energy centers and how they affected our day-to-day lives. Through the assignments, workbook, and classes, my fellow students and I learned techniques to clear and open those energy centers. It was all brand new to me. (If chakras are new to you too, this book will lead you right along.)

I began to recognize that my flawed approach to achieving true happiness would never be achieved by my doing. One of my earliest lessons came in the form of a simple understanding: I am a human BEING, not a human DOING. Twenty-eight years later, I am a changed woman. I am a master teacher of the chakra energy system. I have personally worked with and trained thousands of people about what the chakra energies are, how they function, what we can benefit from knowing about them and working with them.

Why am I telling you this story?

Because if you look at my life now, compared to the dark place I was in back then, I can trace that transformation back to what I did in 1991—working with my chakras. That one decision made a greater impact than I could have imagined, and it can do the same for you. Today's world can seem intense, hectic, depressing, and even scary. So many people are living in the kind of desperation that I did all those years ago. Even if you're not personally in a desperate place, you could easily look around and wonder what to do about the mess that is humanity these days. I speak from experience when I say: Working with your chakra energy system holds the key. Whatever you are meant to fully live, whatever you came to the planet to experience, you can find it by consciously working with your chakra energy. As you do, you will become balanced, aware, and joyful, even with today's world swirling around you. My story invites you to go from where you are now to a place more amazing than you've imagined for yourself. All you have to do is take a step on the path of awakening.

Finding Intuitive Healing Gifts

• • • • • • •

From the very origin of your life, your energy system embodies every thought and emotion and imprints them into your energy field. These become part of your chakra energy. Allowing limiting beliefs and negative repressed emotions to remain in your energy field can eventually materialize into illness, disease, and life crisis. As you clear this interference and open your chakra energy, you tap into a vital life force energy that sustains you in living a life of affluence, ease, and joy.

The more healing and awakening you experience, the more your intuitive gifts can expand. That was definitely the case for me. In 1991, I learned about the seven chakras and became certified in Reiki—a practice of helping people heal their personal energy system through placing hands on certain energy centers. I studied John Bradshaw's work on the inner child. In 1994, I earned my Rapid Eye Therapy certification. I took formal steps toward study and certification, but when I launched my intuitive healing practice as a life coach and healer in 1994, additional, unexpected intuitive abilities also showed up. My reputation grew as my clients experienced profound results in a short time. I offered live trainings to others in the work of energy healing and chakra energy healing.

While working with people energetically, I discovered that I connect with people's emotional experience and psychological plane. In other words, I have an intuitive ability to see and interpret the psychological, emotional, and physical energy that is creating your upset, illness, life crisis, or limitation. If you share with me the imbalance or discomfort you are dealing with, I intuitively know the limiting belief you carry, the emotional pain where the imbalance originated, the age you took it on, and whether or not this pattern is unresolved generational energy in your family system. I can tune into each of your chakras and tell you whether they are open, closed, murky, or running backwards. How do I know? The energy speaks to me and I know what it is saying. Over the years of honing this gift, I have found that I get intuitive hits that feel like the experience of being talked to. For me, reading energy is a bit like speaking a foreign language. Energy is a language and in the energy healing work I do, I translate it into English. I don't put a story on where the intuition comes from, but it is most definitely a source outside of me. The more I have trusted this knowing and gift and used it, the more accurate it has become.

You also have intuitive gifts. They may not manifest in the same way or to the same degree that mine do, but you can develop them. I was able to hone my gifts to help others by first doing deep work with my own energy systems. Without realizing it at first, I was practicing on myself. Your first step toward being able to help others is to work deeply with your own energy system. As you activate your chakras with this book, you will experience your intuition expanding. Trust that you are being led by the divine as you move forward on the path that is correct for you.

Choosing Your Path

· · · · · · ·

You have the opportunity to wake up to your own inner truth, independent of other people's opinions, outside circumstances, or world events. No matter what is happening around you, your choices and your energy can affect your own reality.

In Margery Williams' book, *The Velveteen Rabbit*, an older, wiser toy tells a newer toy what it means to become Real. The character of the Skin Horse has lived in the nursery for a long time and has seen many other toys come and go. He explains to the Velveteen Rabbit that inner transformation matters more than any outer features.

"What is REAL?" Asked the Rabbit one day, when they were lying side by side near the nursery fender, before Nana came to tidy the room. "Does it mean having things that buzz inside you and a stick-out handle?"

"Real isn't how you are made," said the Skin Horse, "It's a thing that happens to you. When a child loves you for a long, long time, not just to play with, but REALLY loves you, then you become Real."

"Does it hurt?" asked the Rabbit.

"Sometimes," said the Skin Horse for he was always truthful. "When you are Real you don't mind being hurt."

"Does it happen all at once like being wound up," he asked, "or bit by bit?"

"It doesn't happen all at once," said the Skin Horse. "You become. It takes a long time. That's why it doesn't often happen to people who break easily, or have sharp edges or who have to be carefully kept. Generally, by the time you are Real, most of your hair has been loved off and your eyes drop out and you get loose in the joints and very shabby. But these things don't matter at all, because once you are Real you can't be ugly, except to people who don't understand."

"I suppose you are Real?" said the Rabbit, and then he wished he had not said it for he thought the Skin Horse might be sensitive. But the Skin Horse only smiled. "The Boy's Uncle made me Real," he said. "That was a great many years ago; but once you are Real you can't become unreal again. It lasts for always."[1]

Becoming Real is waking up to your own inner truth, no matter what is going on around you or what you think you have to do. In some part of your life, you are staying busy, trying to make yourself feel better about yourself through the things that you do. This leaves your sense of self-worth vulnerable to breaking, so you need to be carefully kept. Every time you do this, you miss the grand opportunity to feel 100% sure of your truth and actively live a life that is created from that truth.

Waking up to my inner truth escaped me in my early adult, mothering days. It took time and work for me to awaken to this truth: There is nothing you have to do to be worthwhile, loved, valued, and significant. This truth can awaken in you, too. In fact, we are all born with this truth already within us, but it just did not get nurtured or acknowledged in our childhoods. The good news is, you can choose to become real on your own. *You* can be the one who does the loving, acknowledging, nurturing, and raising up of the inner truth that you are loved and valuable as you are.

Activating your chakra energy is a powerful way to awaken this truth on all levels of your being. In my experience with chakra healing work, I have found that lying dormant in each of these centers of intelligence are golden gems of truth. When activated, they help us awaken to the truth of who we are and live the life we are meant to live, with our soul purpose guiding us. It's a process of becoming real.

As your guide on this path, I bring you 30 years of experience. After starting my private practice in the 1990s, I launched my first website in 2000, as one of the first authors and healers to go online to teach both the principles and techniques of energy healing. In 2007, I was invited to author an online study course on the chakras. That course became Chakra 7, the most popular chakra healing course ever offered for sale on the internet. It reached well over 3 million people during the years that it was available online.

When I was first offered the opportunity to author and publish the Chakra 7 course, the thought came to me: "Why? There is so much information online about the chakras. Why would we need a new course?" I received this intuitive answer very clearly: "Because you have a practical and easy-to-understand way of teaching this information." This is true. The understanding that I have of the chakra energy system could be considered a modern-day understanding of the influence these energy centers have in our day-to-day lives. In the years since receiving my formal chakra energy training in 1991, I have used my intuitive abilities to tune into this powerful energy system and learn from it. In this book, I offer what I've discovered to you.

Are you ready to get Real with yourself? Are you tired of "doing" life? Are you exhausted by recurring self-esteem issues, self-doubt, and insecurities? I was and I did something about it. I can help you suspend the vicious cycle of self-sabotage. You can expect to get more Real from reading this book. In today's world, that looks like greater health and well-being, a clearer connection with your life purpose, more harmony and love in your relationships, increased wealth and abundance, and the ability to truly create the life you want.

The seven steps in this book are the seven energy centers we will walk through on your path of awakening. Let me take you by the hand and guide you in learning more about this powerful energy so you can start to tap into it for your benefit. In the following pages I have included several sections that you will find helpful, depending on the background you are coming from as a reader. Read the sections that apply to you to help you get the most out of this seven-step journey of awakening your energy and waking up to your true self.

Overview of the Chakra Energy System

· · · · · · ·

Whether you are a beginning or advanced student of the chakras, it will be valuable for you to read my thoughts and understanding of the following functions of the chakra energy system:

- 7 Chakra Energy Location and Placement
- Are There Other Chakras?
- How Do the Chakra Energy Centers Affect Us Personally?
- What Does it Mean When You Say a Chakra Energy Is Closed or Open?
- Stages of Chakra Development
- What Are the Origins of the Chakra Energy Teachings?
- Is There Any Scientific Proof That Chakra Energy Is Real?

7 CHAKRA ENERGY LOCATION AND PLACEMENT

Chakra energy refers to seven powerful energies held in energetic stations that run from the bottom of your torso to the top of your head. We each have seven of these energy centers and they each have a universal theme and purpose to influence our life lessons and experiences. Here is a simplistic summary of the purpose and function of each chakra and where it is placed in our energy system:

Chakra 0: Below the feet.

Chakra 0 is a magnetic plate or field below our feet. It could also be called the first floor for the 1st chakra. You will not find many, if any, teachings about this chakra energy, as it is a new energy system that has only recently presented itself in the last 50 or so years. It is nicknamed the "foot chakra." The foot chakra is the bottom floor of the root chakra and would be both yang and yin in its energy movement—yang, moving outward down into the earth and yin, moving energy up from the earth.

1st Chakra: Underneath the torso in the area of the perineum.

The function of the 1st chakra is to energetically root us to the earth. That is why it is nicknamed the "root chakra." The root chakra is a yang energy with the energy moving outward and down toward the earth.

2nd Chakra: In the middle of the belly or mid-back.

The function of the 2nd chakra is to support us in experiencing pleasure and creativity. It is strongly aligned with our sexual pleasure and the birthing of new ideas. It is nicknamed the "sacral" or "creation chakra." The creation chakra is a yang energy, creating a drive and desire to create.

3rd Chakra: Just below the sternum, above the belly button and mid-back.

The function of the 3rd chakra is to instill us with a sense of authentic power and will. It is nicknamed the "power chakra." The power chakra is a yang energy, with the energy moving outward to take action in the world.

4th Chakra: Middle of the chest and space between the shoulder blades.

The function of the 4th chakra is to support us in expressing and receiving the energy of love and gratitude. It is nicknamed the "heart chakra." The heart chakra is both a yin and yang energy, with the energy moving inward for us to receive first, and then outward as we give.

5th Chakra: The larynx or middle of the throat on both sides of the neck.

The function of the 5th chakra is to support us in thinking and vocally expressing our truth with confidence and ease. It is nicknamed the "throat chakra." The throat chakra is a yang energy, flowing outward as we express ourselves with our voice.

6th Chakra: The middle of the forehead and upper backside of the head.

The function of the 6th chakra is to assist us in developing and using our intuitive knowing with confidence. It is nicknamed the "intuitive chakra" or "the third eye." The intuitive chakra is a yin energy, with the energy moving inward as we seek insight and strengthen our inner knowing.

The 7th Chakra: The top or crown of the head.

The function of the 7th chakra is to connect us with spirit and the divine. It is nicknamed the "crown chakra." The crown chakra is both yin and yang, with the energy first moving into us from heaven, then down through all the chakras below it, connecting us to the earth then back up again through the crown chakra, back up to heaven.

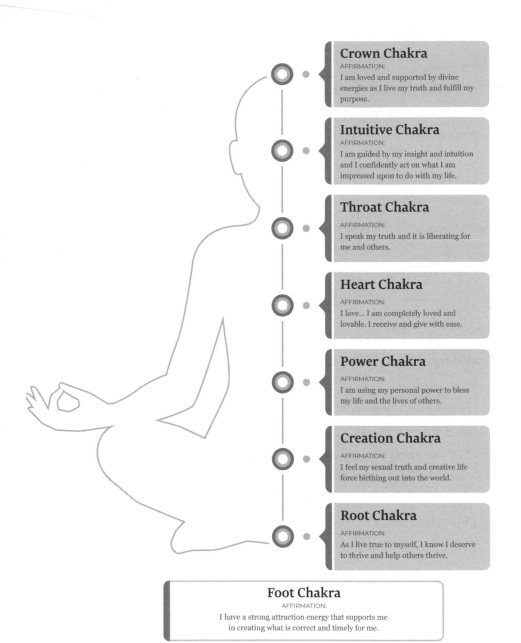

Crown Chakra
AFFIRMATION:
I am loved and supported by divine energies as I live my truth and fulfill my purpose.

Intuitive Chakra
AFFIRMATION:
I am guided by my insight and intuition and I confidently act on what I am impressed upon to do with my life.

Throat Chakra
AFFIRMATION:
I speak my truth and it is liberating for me and others.

Heart Chakra
AFFIRMATION:
I love... I am completely loved and lovable. I receive and give with ease.

Power Chakra
AFFIRMATION:
I am using my personal power to bless my life and the lives of others.

Creation Chakra
AFFIRMATION:
I feel my sexual truth and creative life force birthing out into the world.

Root Chakra
AFFIRMATION:
As I live true to myself, I know I deserve to thrive and help others thrive.

Foot Chakra
AFFIRMATION:
I have a strong attraction energy that supports me in creating what is correct and timely for me.

In the coming chapters, you will receive more in-depth understanding of each of these chakras and see how they are functioning in your personal life. I will also share energetic exercises you can do to activate and strengthen each one.

ARE THERE OTHER CHAKRAS BESIDES THE PRIMARY SEVEN?

Yes, we have more energy centers fluctuating energy all over our bodies, but these primary seven are the mainframe of our personal energy system and have the most power in influencing how our energy is running as a whole system. If the chakra energy system is not healthy, your entire energy system will not run at its optimal capacity. This includes your auric field. Your auric field is the energy container that you are held by. In everyday language, we would call it your personal space—the 6-8-foot range around you that you can sense, even though you can't see anything there. This auric field can become distorted or collapse on you. Imbalance in your chakras can lead to your meridian energy or energetic pathways becoming stuck, dormant, or running backwards. An issue in your chakras can compromise your spiritual, mental, and emotional energy bodies, as well as your physical constitution. Even though you are comprised of a complex system of energy centers, it is worthwhile for you to focus on these seven, as they affect the whole system.

HOW DO THE CHAKRA ENERGY CENTERS AFFECT US?

Your chakra energy is a powerful energetic influence in your life. In *Anatomy of the Spirit,* Caroline Myss describes the function of chakras as follows: "Every thought and experience you've ever had in your life gets filtered through these chakra databases. Each event is recorded into your cells…"[2] Each of the seven chakras contributes to having a healthy subtle energy system. The chakras are moving cylinders of energy that breathe, pulling energy in and expelling energy out. Each chakra spins at a particular vibratory rate that customizes the energy to have a specific effect for us. The individual chakra breathes in life force energy, transforms the energy into a particular vibratory rate that then expels that energy to support us in creating an abundance of life experiences within that chakra's specific function. In other words, chakra energy feeds your life force energy.

The root chakra has the slowest vibratory rate and the frequency of each chakra increases to a higher vibratory rate as you move up from the root chakra to the crown chakra. Think of playing a scale from the lower notes to the higher notes on a piano keyboard. When the energy of a chakra is not healthy, it can attract to you unhealthy, dysfunctional experiences that are not enjoyable. It is a missing note on the keyboard. The chakras work independently and as a whole system. When one chakra is weak, the entire system is weakened.

Even though you are not aware of it (just as you are not consciously aware of all of your biological systems functioning throughout the day), your chakra energy is affecting you in every moment. When the chakras are healthy and doing their job, they help us receive life force energy that affects every aspect of our life. They also support our physiology in working properly. Here are the themes or specific areas of our lives that each chakra affects:

- Foot chakra: Standing in our truth
- 1st chakra: Rooted in our truth
- 2nd chakra: Pleasuring in our truth
- 3rd chakra: Acting from our truth
- 4th chakra: Loving our truth

- 5th chakra: Speaking our truth
- 6th chakra: Knowing our truth
- 7th chakra: Seeing our truth

Keywords that identify each chakra's function in the order of their placement (starting at the 1st chakra) are: rooted, pleasure, act, love, speak, see, and know. An easy way to remember the function of each chakra is to memorize the following mantra:

- I stand in my truth.
- I am rooted in my truth.
- I pleasure in my truth.
- I act on my truth.
- I love my truth.
- I speak my truth.
- I know my truth.
- I see my truth.

When our chakra energy centers are not healthy, we are compromised and experience that compromise as dysfunctional life experiences or an unhealthy body. When you have a weak, dysfunctional, or closed chakra, that chakra is not breathing, contributing, or playing its role in sustaining your life force in a healthy energetic balance. In your muscular system, if one muscle isn't working well, another muscle has to make up the difference. It is the same for your chakra energy. If one chakra is not doing its job, another chakra has to make up the difference, causing unstable life force energy, which can lead to imbalances in physical, mental, or emotional health.

Here is an example of how imbalanced chakra energy centers can manifest as real-world challenges. Susan, an online student of mine, suffered from an extreme case of fibromyalgia for several decades. She started to have symptoms in her early 20s. At that time in her life, she was engaged to a man she thought was the love of her life, only to find out he was unfaithful to her and involved with another woman. Honesty and commitment are important to Susan—as they should be to anyone planning to marry! In her case, she had come from a family where her father had not been faithful to her mother. So, this energetic pattern and residual energy had been set up earlier in her life and preceded her relationship experience. In her healing process, Susan discovered her subconscious belief that, "Men are not faithful." This deep belief and underlying energy had compromised her 2nd and 4th chakras.

The 2nd chakra, the creation chakra, supports us in having a pleasurable life—in particular, enjoying sexual pleasure. When a partner is not sexually faithful, our own 2nd chakra energy cannot fully open and blossom during a sexual experience with our partner. The 4th chakra, the heart chakra, supports us in fully connecting with the energy of love with our partner. Our heart chakras actually bond, creating a strong connection that feeds each of our chakras in our partnership. When one partner is not telling the truth, our heart chakra experiences this. If our mind overrides this inner knowing to try to believe the person, the 4th chakra is blocked. The 2nd chakra influences our lymphatic system and the 4th chakra influences our circulatory system, which are both systems of flow in our body. Our chakra energy centers are trying to communicate with us all the time, and if we ignore their energetic promptings, they grow weak, become imbalanced, and stop supporting us.

In Susan's case, her weak and dysfunctional 2nd and 4th chakras were compensated for by her 3rd chakra, which ran more energy to counteract the blocks. The 3rd chakra is the power chakra and when we are not in a healthy relationship, our power chakra is affected. This energy helps us use our will to make sure we have healthy boundaries and experience mutual respect in an intimate relationship. When it is forced into overactivity due to an imbalance, the energy of anger builds up. If this goes unacknowledged and we do not use our throat chakra to express anger about an injustice, the body has to account for that anger.

In Susan's case, her compromised 2nd and 4th chakras and overactive 3rd chakra energy contributed to her body being compromised with the condition of fibromyalgia. When chakra energy is compromised, the body creates a sign in the form of disease and imbalance. In Susan's life, that physical sign was fibromyalgia. As she started to work on her 2nd and 4th chakra energy centers, Susan's health improved.

As you continue through this book, consider the events of your life. Consider the imbalances you experience or the things you would like to heal. Ask yourself: How are my chakra energy systems affecting me? Trust that you will receive answers and intuitive impressions that lead you to healing and activation of your higher self.

HOW DOES OUR CHAKRA ENERGY BECOME WEAK, DYSFUNCTIONAL, OR CLOSED?

Improper development, life trauma at any age, poor diet, and toxic environments can leave your chakra energy centers blocked, imbalanced, running backward, frozen, or even misplaced in your subtle energy field. This just means the energy is not moving as it's designed to move and flow.

Imagine a vortex or a cone of energy extending from the area in your body where the chakra is located. For example, picture 2nd chakra energy as a cone of spiraling energy coming off your abdomen and lower back. It is like a spinning cylinder. If it is blocked, it would look smashed down with no spiraling effect. If it is stagnant or frozen, it would look droopy and floppy with no movement. If it is running backward or spastic, it would look like a spiral that has a spastic movement to it.

I'll share a personal example to show how this can play out in your life. My 2nd chakra did not have a chance to properly develop in my childhood, due to childhood sexual abuse. I had an unhealthy and conflicted relationship with my father—the original male who I was supposed to create a healthy and appropriate bond with. The male who helped give me life also played the role of perpetrator, which had a deep and long-term wounding effect on my 2nd chakra, causing it to freeze and lock up. My traumatized, frozen 2nd chakra manifested over the years for me as resistance to sexual intimacy, PTSD triggered during sexual activity with my husband, an inability to experience orgasm well into my marriage, along with other challenges. It took me decades to find the correct tools to heal this energy system so that I now have the benefit of enjoying my sexual creative energy in a manner that brings me pleasure.

Once I started to really experience the benefit of my 2nd chakra healing, my sexual experience improved and my creative juices started to open and flow. A look at my creative output over my professional years shows evidence of this chakra healing and getting healthy. Since my early 40s, I have written six books and this is my seventh. I also created the work I am the most well-known for online: Energy Profiling, Dressing Your Truth, and The Child Whisperer. That is a tremendous amount of creative output in 17 years. I attribute it to the healing of my 2nd chakra that opened my creative energy and supported me in creating this body of work.

Like me, you may have a chakra (or several) that are stagnant or frozen due to trauma. Most people have at least some degree of chakra wounding that needs to be addressed. Fortunately, chakra energy is a constantly moving, living energy force that can change in the blink of an eye! Any chakra could be fully functioning, open, and healthy in certain environments, around people you feel safe with. In the same 24 hours, it can change to be dysfunctional, blocked, or closed if you are in a place with people you do not feel safe or true to yourself around. This is good news because it means you can make changes in your life that will immediately open and activate your chakras. As you do, you will unlock powerful energy to support you.

STAGES OF CHAKRA DEVELOPMENT

When we are born, our root chakra starts to form. Each chakra energy center then develops over our childhood and teenage years. Depending on their development in our early years, these energy centers either grow stronger, stay stagnant, or get out of balance. If you did not receive the support for your chakras to properly develop in your early childhood years, that chakra stays stuck in a holding pattern which compromises you in that area of life. The following chart shows the ages that each chakra is developed as we move through our childhood and teen years:

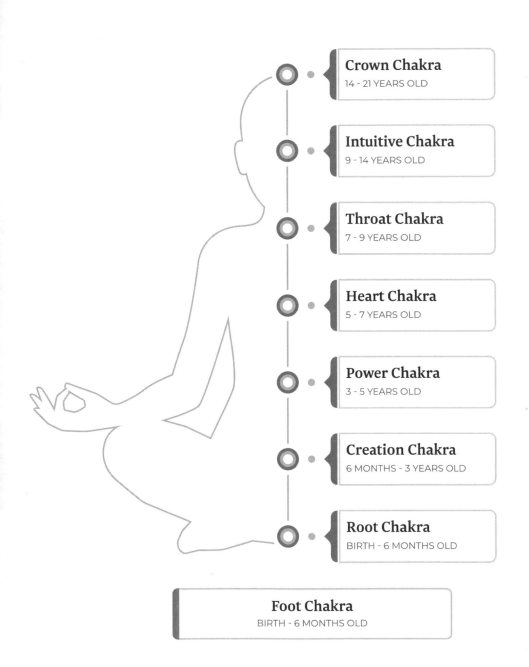

Crown Chakra
14 - 21 YEARS OLD

Intuitive Chakra
9 - 14 YEARS OLD

Throat Chakra
7 - 9 YEARS OLD

Heart Chakra
5 - 7 YEARS OLD

Power Chakra
3 - 5 YEARS OLD

Creation Chakra
6 MONTHS - 3 YEARS OLD

Root Chakra
BIRTH - 6 MONTHS OLD

Foot Chakra
BIRTH - 6 MONTHS OLD

1st Chakra Development: The Root Chakra. Birth–6 months

During our first few months of life, our physical body is developing and we begin to form our first connection with our parents and our surroundings. The level of care and support we receive for our physical and emotional needs sets into motion our patterns of how valuable we feel we are. If our needs are met in this time period, we develop the deep belief that, "I am valuable and my needs are valuable." If we are not a priority to our parents or caregivers, or if they hold any form of resentment that distracts them from caring for us in their heart, we develop a false belief of, "I am not valuable and my needs are not important." Clearing blocks and activating this energy center supports you in feeling like you belong and your needs are worthwhile.

**2nd Chakra Development: The Creation Chakra.
Ages 6 months–3 years**

During this stage our feelings awaken, as well as our creative responses to the people and situations around us. We start to develop a perception about our feelings and whether or not it is safe to express them. The creation chakra is the energy center that supports our sense of having the right to be creative and expressive.

Our parents may inadvertently teach us that some feelings are not okay. If we are exposed to dysfunctional displays of emotion, we will sense and later believe that certain feelings are bad. Or to survive dysfunctional family environments, we model our own behavior after our parents' dysfunctional behavior. We are sensory perceptive as small children and can take on the energy of feelings that are not accounted for or managed well by our parents or caregivers. We do all we can as children to try and bring balance to our environment, even absorb the feelings of our family members as our own. Clearing blocks and activating this energy center supports you in finding pleasure and creative fulfillment.

3rd Chakra Development: The Power Chakra. Ages 3–5

During this stage, we become aware of the world around us. We start to perceive who we are and how much power we have, based on the reactions of the adults around us. We learn the power of saying yes and no, and whether or not those declarations are welcomed by adults. We start to form ideas about who we are and the rules we need to live by that are put upon us from others.

If we are criticized, we tend to develop a pattern of criticizing ourselves and feeling like we never measure up. We also tend to attract people in our adult life who replicate this experience. We start to form an opinion of ourselves that we then carry into the rest of our lives. If we are praised, loved, and encouraged, we tend to recreate this behavior. These early experiences develop our view of our personal power and ability to relate to others. Clearing blocks and activating this energy center allows you to claim your power back and take action.

4th Chakra Development: The Heart Chakra. Ages 5–7

During this stage, we move into our heart energy. Our circle of influence begins to expand beyond our family of origin. We start to spend more time with peers, friends, teachers, media, books, and more.

If our family of origin is a system where everyone is honored, where there is a sense of being allies and friends, and where giving and receiving are balanced, then the natural cycle of giving and receiving will easily be created in our additional relationships. If we experienced that someone has to make a sacrifice for another family member to "get their way," we will be out of balance with the natural cycle of giving and receiving.

When we are children, our heart energy is completely open. As we experience pain and wounding of our true selves, we create blocks in this energy center to protect ourselves or try to stop the pain. These blocks also restrict our unconditional love and our connection to divine energy that feeds into our heart center. If we experience heart energy being shut down or blocked in our family of origin, then giving, receiving, and creating loving bonds in our adult relationships can become challenging or nonexistent. Clearing blocks and activating this energy center allows us to experience our natural, childlike state of self-acceptance, love, and trust in others.

5th Chakra Development: The Throat Chakra. Ages 7–9

During this span of years, we are starting to say what we think and feel. We gain a better sense of how others react to us. Speaking is one way we manifest what we want and need. If our family of origin supports and respects our verbal expressions and engages us in encouraging conversation, we will feel it's safe to share our true self. If we are raised in a dysfunctional family environment where communicating our ideas, opinions, values, wants, and needs is not encouraged, or is even shamed and punished, we will have blocks in this chakra energy.

If we are not allowed to speak authentically as children, blocks or inhibitions in self-expression follow us into our adult life. These blocks manifest as communication problems and people-pleasing tendencies in speaking what others want to hear. Clearing these blocks and activating this energy center will help you recognize what you want and need, as well as energize your voice so you can consistently speak what is true for you, instead of what you think others want you to say.

6th Chakra Development: The Intuition Chakra. Ages 9–14

During this stage, our visions and goals for our future adult life start to form. We start to consider the possibilities of what we want to do, who we want to be, and what we want out of life. We start to experiment with life and try new ways of being ourselves. We do this with self-expression, fashion, and hobbies. If we still feel a need to please and accommodate our parents, we will do what they want and this energy center will not be energized. If this energy center is still blocked in our adult lives, we will find it difficult to feel inspired or moved to do what we want; we will feel overall malaise or depression about life. Clearing blocks and activating this energy center will bring new zeal and awareness to who we are, what we want, and will invigorate extra-sensory gifts and powers.

7th Chakra Development: The Crown Chakra. Ages 14–21

During this stage, more energy pours through this energy center from divine sources. This energy holds the awareness of our own purpose and our own guiding principles. In this timeframe, we are maturing into our own experience with the divine and how we choose to experience our spirituality. If we are encouraged to follow guidance from a higher source, and not only the rules of our parents, we will develop a connection to the divine and a trust that we are worthy of spiritual help. If we are forced to choose our parents' religious and spiritual philosophies, we experience religion as a controlling authority over us and may choose to not participate anymore in an organized religion.

At this stage of life, we are stepping onto our life path and our soul lessons. We may be programmed with so much fear that we choose to do what our family and parents expect of us when it comes to our religious and spiritual beliefs. However, if we have not chosen those values and beliefs for ourselves, we will be met with inner turmoil and resistance in some manner in our lives. This stage of life can be a time of struggle and confusion or a time of the activation of our higher purpose with grace and ease. Clearing blocks and activating this energy center supports you in finding connection with something higher than yourself.

What happened in your life during these stages? Were you safe and supported? If you were, then your chakra energy systems would have developed properly. Most people have one or more chakra energies that need attention in adulthood, due to improper development in their childhood. One of the primary benefits of working with your chakra energy now as an adult is to make up the difference for any underdeveloped chakras that compromise your life. The information in this book and other chakra resources I offer are designed to assist you in making up that difference and achieving balance.

HOW DOES THIS BOOK CONNECT TO THE ORIGIN OF CHAKRA ENERGY TEACHINGS?

We could fill a whole book with information on the historical and religious origins of the chakras. These origins date back to 1500-500 BC in ancient Hindu texts called the Vedas.[3] The word *chakra* has Sanskrit roots meaning *wheel* or *cycle*.[4]

Historically, ancient chakra practices were connected to religious practice that involved meditation and mantras, with no reference to psychological, emotional, or physical states. In fact, ancient Eastern teachings involving chakra (or cakra) energy refer to numerous energy bodies and systems that have become popular in modern-day Western cultures, not just the seven I share in this book.

Outlining the full picture of chakra history is beyond the scope of this book. This is meant to be a practical guide, not a historical text. However, if you are interested in reading more about how Eastern chakras found their way into Western culture, you can research mentions of chakra energy in writings by Swiss psychologist Carl Jung and American mythologist Joseph Campbell. Both of those writers cited John Woodroffe, an Indian high court judge who wrote about chakra energy in the early 1900s.[5] Two modern works that have been widely read that have influenced the popularity of studying the chakra system in our modern times are *Wheels of Life* by Anodea Judith[6] and *Anatomy of the Spirit* by Carolyn Myss.[7] I recommended both books.

I would classify modern-day texts and teachings of the chakra energy system in the genre of self-help rather than religious study. This is useful to know for someone who may be worried that studying the chakra energy is in direct conflict with their religious practices.

I classify the chakra information that I personally teach as a practical approach to help you improve your overall life experience. In addition to helping you activate the seven chakra energy centers, this book also teaches you about a shift that has been occurring in the chakra system since the 1960s to the current time, with an even bigger shift occurring since we entered the new millennium of 2000. My work is original and comes from my ability to read and interpret chakra energy.

We are currently in a process of awakening at the time of this writing, sometimes at such a pace that it seems surreal and that we are living in a madhouse. The misdeeds of the past and hidden secrets are being brought to light. Vile and violent acts by a few cause great harm to many. If you've ever looked at the news on the world stage and thought, "What is happening?" you're not alone. Here's what's happening: We are collectively getting an energetic upgrade and the process is uncomfortable, especially for those who are not mindful or conscious of the shift.

In my book, *Mastering Affluence*, I describe the phenomenon of an energetic effect that is occurring on the planet called the Schuman

Resonance Factor.[8] The Schuman Resonance measures the vibration of the energy of planet Earth. The earth's vibrational frequency has been measured as substantially increasing since 2005. With the vibration of the planet rising, chakra energies—our primary energy centers—are being activated and opened to higher states of energy. We are basically being called up to live our truth and account for all the creations that are in conflict with that truth.

People's heart chakras are turning on and crown chakras are being flooded with light and truth. In a world where that is happening, the violence in this world seems even harsher and more unacceptable. The unacceptable is becoming more unacceptable. The contrast between acts of darkness and acts of light is ever more discernible. The light and the good will prevail; it's just taking us some time to get there. Your children's children are being born with their chakras active and operating. Those who will save this world from its own craziness and confusion are starting to arrive. In the grand scale of the human experience, all will be well. So I invite you to focus on the mini-reality you are creating to make the best version of your life available. Understanding and working with your chakra energy will assist you in doing that.

IS THERE ANY SCIENTIFIC EVIDENCE THAT CHAKRA ENERGY IS REAL?

Honestly, that depends on what kind of evidence you are looking for. I will share with you some research I've found interesting, but before I do, I'd like you to consider the experience of love. Scientific instruments cannot measure the experience or expression of love. The closest researchers have gotten to verifying love is "real" is by measuring the chemical reactions in the brain and the endocrine system. This could be compared to looking for physical evidence of a chakra energy in the pineal gland. The pineal gland has been associated with the intuitive, "third eye" chakra in numerous teachings for decades. Pineal gland research does show that this gland responds to light and has a quartz-like quality to it.[9] But that does not "prove" the existence of a chakra energy any more than brain activity "proves" the existence of love.

The esoteric, mystical, and metaphysical experiences of life are not given much attention in scientific circles. Because of that, there is little research on chakra energy. The research that *can* be found often refers to the ability to measure the human body's electromagnetic field and its vibratory frequency. In the 1970s, Dr. Hiroshi Motoyama—both a scientist and a Shinto priest—developed a device called The Chakra Instrument, meant to measure chakra energy.[10] In the 1980s and 90s, Dr. Valerie Hunt at UCLA researched and recorded radiation coming from the body at the seven chakra sites.[11] As our scientific tools become more sophisticated, additional research is starting to pop up in scientific spaces. In 2005, a book called *The Scientific Basis of Integrative Medicine* examined current medical research alongside subtle energy bodies.[12] And an article in 2013 in *The Journal of Consciousness Exploration and Research* reported on attempts to map chakras using electrical current and meditation.[13] If you are like me, the scientific research is fun to read, but not necessary for you to know and feel it is correct to proceed in your studies of the chakras. You feel called to study this information, or you have an interest in the metaphysical experiences of life as a hobby. You may have experienced your own mystical journey that this book will help to validate.

If you need scientific evidence to "buy into all of this," I invite you to look at your life and consider how many other concepts you have taken on as truth without scientific evidence to back them. For example, if you believe in God, you put your faith and trust in the divine without irrefutable scientific evidence to back it. If you are secular in your beliefs and need scientific evidence to feel confident that this is information you can trust, I encourage you to treat your chakra study as a hobby, like cooking. Don't put this information in a role where you have to steadfastly believe that it is true in order to learn more. Just enjoy the learning and if any of it adds more joy to your life, bonus. Take it!

Chakra Study for the Beginner Student

· · · · · · ·

If you are new to learning about chakra energy, that is actually a great place to be! I teach a more modern-day, practical understanding of the chakra energy system and how it affects our lives in today's world of great change. I invite you to read this book with the intention of personal application. As I share my personal experience with chakra energy, look for your own experiences. Chakra energy is already affecting your life, whether you're aware of it or not. By putting your awareness on the effects of chakra energy in your life, you will activate their energy and create a life that supports you better.

If you're a beginner, it's actually fortunate you have nothing to compare my approach with. If that sounds funny, let me clarify with a story. When my oldest daughter, Jenny, was in her early teens, I started to notice that she had a natural talent for singing. One evening, while my parents were visiting, they asked her to sing for them and they were impressed with her talent. My father told her if she found a voice teacher, he would pay for her training.

That set the energy in motion. In the next few weeks, and as a result of certain connections, Jenny was put in touch with one of the most recognized voice teachers in our state. This voice teacher was not taking on new students and rarely worked with singers as young as Jenny. But when you have a natural gift, the chakra energy connected to that gift plays a part in attracting the opportunities and events that will support you in using it. In Jenny's case it was the 5th chakra—her throat chakra. Our energies are so powerful, they will override the logic of what "should happen" and open up the space for what wants to happen. Jenny was given the chance to audition for Betty Jean and Betty Jean fell in love with Jenny and her voice.

She asked Jenny if she had previous training. Jenny said no. Betty Jean was thrilled. She knew she would not have to undo or work with pre-existing influences and that she could train Jenny's voice to be true to who Jenny is.

That is the case for you as a beginner. You don't need to worry that you don't know enough or that all of this is new for you. You have set the energy in motion by picking up this book, and coming fresh to the information in this book will be an asset for you. Being a chakra newbie is a good thing. You have some exciting things to learn that will change your life for the better if you put them into practice.

Chakra Study for the Advanced Student

· · · · · · ·

If you have been a previous student of chakra energy, thank you for letting me add to your current knowledge of this energy system. Whatever background you come from, I encourage you to collect more insights and tools and choose to not make reading my book a comparative study of what you already know.

In your other study, you have probably noticed that those who teach the workings of esoteric energies each have their own unique perspective on these energies. You can see similarities and differences between what they teach. The goal I hope for you is to continue to add to your growing knowledge of the chakras to support you in creating more affluence, ease, and joy in your life.

What you will learn from me (that may differ from other sources) is information on the changing and evolving function and influence of the chakras in our experience in today's world. For example, most sources on the chakras universally agree that each chakra expresses a certain color ray.

1st Chakra: Red
2nd Chakra: Orange
3rd Chakra: Yellow
4th Chakra: Green
5th Chakra: Blue
6th Chakra: Indigo
7th Chakra: Violet

This list has been the common reference of our chakra colors for some time now. Yet, we live at a time when we are gaining more energetic independence and no longer being held by a collective energy system. As a result, we are each becoming independently our own chakra color ray expression. As mentioned before, I am personally tuned into energy and able to interpret it, and I have noticed in my clients' experience variations from the typical chart, such as a pink ray in the heart chakra when their heart was healing, brown or black in the root chakra when the individual is working on more grounding and pulling in multiple color rays at one time. I've seen crystalline quartz energy flooding a person's crown chakra.

It's not necessary for you to be able to see personal color rays in order to understand the evolving nature of the chakras. What *is* important for you personally is to not get too locked into what you already know about chakra energy that you cannot accept something new. If you come across something in this book that doesn't seem to match what you've learned before, consider it as a possibility. I trust that you will incorporate whatever part of this book is correct for you in your personal path to awakening. Stay open. If you're an advanced chakra student, I already know that you will!

Chakra Study for the Religious Student

● ● ● ● ● ● ●

What I present to you, I categorize as self-help materials. Never would I suggest or encourage you to replace your religious beliefs and practices with what you are learning from me. I respect the fact that your religious experience is a foundation on which you build your life. As I moved into studying this genre over 30 years ago, I felt very much guided by what I experience as the holy spirit in what I was led to study and learn. As you seek divine guidance from God and the divine, you too will be guided to what is timely and appropriate for you to learn.

Even though the teachings of the chakras do have ties to Eastern religions, in my approach, I teach you about a powerful energy system that is affecting you every day of your life. The more you know about it, the more you can work with it and reap the benefits of what these energies influence day to day.

You are not replacing your religious beliefs with what you learn from me. You are adding powerful self-help tools to your tool kit to support you in creating wellness and a thriving life. Use this book as a guide, as you would any self-help book, choosing to draw from it what feels right for you. Put aside what does not ring true for you. Pray for guidance of the holy spirit as you read and seek to understand the tools and principles taught here. I trust that you are your own spiritual authority and I would never presume to take that role from you.

As you reflect on whether or not this material this feels correct for you to study, the following stories of some of my students could be helpful to you.

Melissa shared: "I am a religious person. I will admit that I even approached energy healing with some caution as I sought to gain clarity and understanding and decide if it could coincide with my religious beliefs as I understand from the Bible, which is my chosen source of life guidance. My feeling is I don't want to do anything ever that would offend the God I love and honor. Energy Profiling very much harmonized with that, as I believe in creation, that we are created from the elements of the earth and that we are obviously living, energetic beings. So that "checked out" ok with me. Personally, I will take a similar approach to chakra healing as I did to energy healing and see how I feel about it. I think knowledge and education are vital so thank you for opening this opportunity for us to learn more!"

Lachelle shared: "Growing up, I came from a very strict, conservative religious background. A lot of my beliefs were there because someone said so! Anything that wasn't in the Bible went under a heading of "you better leave it alone." My husband & I have discussed that much of what we now hold as truth would not be accepted by many of our friends. However, when you compare the teachings to what you teach, they are the same! Here's an example: Visualization, affirmations and meditation—the book of Psalms teaches us to meditate on God's Word, which is meditation practice, but it doesn't call it that. We are energetic beings. There is much I feel we have put unworthy labels on due to our lack of understanding. I'm excited to learn more—to learn truth."

Over the years, I have heard from people that studying energy and natural healing were somehow a contradiction to the religious practices they embraced. I had some of those same fears myself at first, yet my desire to heal opened me up to this new opportunity. Learning from Eastern practices and modalities actually helped me understand my own religious and spiritual beliefs more clearly.

It has been my experience that when you honor your religious beliefs as you study metaphysical teachings and alternative healing practices, you create a unique and personal healing experience that will help you create a deeper understanding and connection with your own religious beliefs and practices.

Chakra Study for the Secular Student

· · · · · · ·

As you will learn in this book, we are being uprooted from cultural energetic holdings to walk our own life paths of inner knowing and belief. For that reason, it would be challenging to find a book that honored all the unique worldviews, spiritual views, and non-spiritual views at this time in history. If you do not adhere to a specific religious experience—from agnostic to not having a belief in God—I respect your experience and worldview. I will be honest: you will need to make more adaptations to my teachings in this book than anyone else.

The origin of the chakra energy system dates back to 1500—500 BC, to Hindu religious books of knowledge called the Vedas. But today's teachings of the chakra energy system would be classified in the metaphysical self-help genre. To benefit from the teachings I share in this book, please adapt any spiritually oriented language to your preferences. You may feel more supported by replacing words like *spirit* or *divine* with *nature*, *universe*, or your *all-knowing self*. As you make the adaptations you prefer, you will gain timely personal insights from this book.

The Chakra System for Planet Earth

· · · · · · ·

The Hawaiian Islands are a unique island chain in the middle of the Pacific Ocean. They are unique because the seven islands appear to stand alone, nearly 1,300 miles from the next visible island chain in the South Pacific. It has been speculated that these seven islands represent the chakra system of the planet, with each island resonating with one of the seven chakra energies.[14] For those of us who agree that the Hawaiian islands are an archetype of chakra energy, visiting the islands can help you activate and amplify your connection to your own truth and the earth.

If you have had the opportunity to travel to the islands of Hawaii, then you have observed firsthand that each island has its own unique and powerful energy. I have had the blessing of visiting and even living part-time in Hawaii since I was 12 years old. I find this serendipitous, as the powerful healing energies support me in fulfilling my mission of helping others live their truth.

It is interesting to see how chakra energies show up in nature. Observing a few details about each Hawaiian island will give you another reference point and mental image to support your chakra learning in this book. Here is a brief overview of each of the Hawaiian islands and the chakra energy it is an archetype for:

1st Chakra or Root Chakra—Hawaii Island

Root chakra energy is associated with being grounded to the earth as our support system of life. The Big Island of Hawaii was formed by five volcanoes.[15] It is primarily composed of the red and black energy of the lava that created it. The island of Hawaii is also the biggest island, just as the root chakra is one of the most active energy centers for humankind.

2nd Chakra or Creation Chakra—Maui

The second chakra is associated with creativity, procreation, and the energy of passion. The island of Maui is a "resort" island. It is known for its lovely beachfront resorts that attract couples and honeymooners. Between the months of November and April, humpback whales migrate from Alaskan waters to breed and give birth in the water just off the shores of Maui.[16]

3rd Chakra or Power Chakra—Lanai

The power chakra is the center of our personal strength and willpower. The island of Lanai is known as the "pineapple island" for all the pineapple production that used to occur there. James Dole, founder of Dole Pineapple, purchased Lanai in 1922 and at the highest point of pineapple production, 75% of the world's pineapple was produced there.[17] The world *lanai* means "conquest of the sun" which suggests a powerful, warm energy.

4th Chakra or Heart Chakra—Molokai

The heart chakra is the energy of receiving and giving love and compassion. The island of Molokai is known as the "Heart of Hawaii." It is the only island that is largely untouched by tourism and stays connected to the heart of Hawaiian history.[18] It is a quiet and peaceful island environment.

The 5th Chakra or Throat Chakra—Oahu

The throat chakra is connected to our ability to communicate and express our truth with confidence and without apology. Of all the Hawaiian islands, the island of Oahu is the most populated and most visited by tourists. It is known as the "gathering place."[19] The government of the state of Hawaii operates there, making Oahu the voice of the islands.

The 6th Chakra or Intuitive Chakra—Kauai

The intuitive chakra is associated with intuition and inspiration. The island of Kauai is known as a place for retreat and meditation. It has maintained a rural, low-key environment. It is known as the "garden island" due to all the rain and growth, which can be associated with the way intuitive insights help us grow and thrive when we follow them.

The 7th Chakra or Crown Chakra—Niihau

The crown chakra connects us with our divine truth and supports us in fulfilling our highest purpose. The island of Niihau is actually a private island. It is a beautiful, pristine environment, untouched by modern-day developments of society. It can be compared to the pure, white light of the crown chakra.

The Old Energy and the
New Energy of the Chakras

• • • • • • •

Just as you are about to go through an awakening by reading Part Two of this book, the chakras are going through a shift. You're feeling this shift and seeing its effects play out, whether you realize it or not. It is my experience that the more my thinking mind knows what's happening to me at a subtle energy level, the more I consciously can participate and experience smoother, more balanced transitions in the lessons I am moving through.

We are in a transition between an old energy and a new energy that affects our experience as humans. The old energy influenced what used to be the norm for the experience of humanity. The new energy is what we are coming into experiencing individually and as a humanity. In this transition, our chakra energy systems are getting "turned on," whether each of us choose into it or not. This shift causes change that can feel uncomfortable and unfamiliar if you don't consciously know what is going on. In fact, all you need to do is turn on the news to see that today's world seems to have gone sideways because many people don't know how to navigate this shift. You can choose to become a conscious manager of your own energy system so that the energetic transition doesn't manage you.

In each section of Part Two, I will share how people experienced the old energy of each chakra and how we are starting to experience the new energy. Not everyone is going through this shift at the same time or in the same way. In fact, some of your older family members may not even fully choose into this process of awakening. Remembering that everyone's experience is unique will support you in making your own choices without making comparisons to others or judgments toward yourself.

As you read Part Two, I encourage you to evaluate yourself. Pay attention to what you notice in your own life experience as you move through the chapters. Pay attention to what is happening in your own chakra energy system. Don't worry about anyone else. Ask yourself: What am I ready to learn? Which lessons are showing up right now that are being energized by my chakra energy system? As you awaken your energy and step into a more powerful, balanced version of yourself, you will naturally help others through this transition to the new energy without even trying. Focus on your own energetic system first.

Your chakra energy is calling to you—are you listening? Let me help you listen and translate the energetic messages that are speaking to you, so you can benefit from all they have to offer. It's time to awaken to the more inspired life that's waiting for you.

Part Two

· · · · · · ·

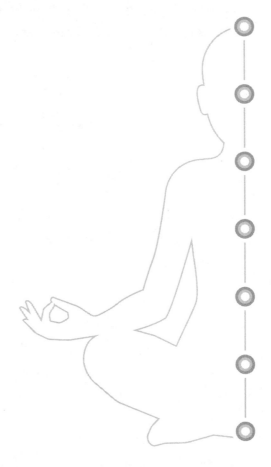

How to Use the Introduction
to Each Chakra

• • • • • • •

In the following chapters, you will learn about each of the chakras in more depth—beginning with the foot chakra and moving all the way up to the crown chakra. Each chapter begins with a list of details about a specific chakra, such as that chakra's location and function. So that you can easily understand these lists, here is a simple explanation of the details you will find at the beginning of the chapters to come.

Location:	This refers to the position of a chakra. Each chakra's energy vibrates in a certain place in relation to your physical body, such as the foot or heart.
Yin/Yang Flow:	The inward or outward quality of movement of a chakra—with yin referring to inward and yang referring to outward.
Universal Color:	The color vibration that a chakra is most often said to express.
Associated Organs and Body Parts:	The body parts commonly associated with each chakra, as well as physical issues that tend to manifest when the chakra is imbalanced.
Function:	The function of a chakra's energy. The energy of each particular chakra will support you in certain aspects of your life, such as connecting you to your purpose or expressing your voice.
Old Energy:	Prior to the 1960s, each chakra's energy influenced people's lives in a particular way. We are shifting away from that energy into a newer energy. Each chapter shares the old energy so that you can see the difference.
New Energy:	The newer, modern-day influence of a chakra's energy in people's lives from 1960 to the present.
If Closed:	When a chakra's energy is weak or dormant, that energy manifests somewhere in your life in relation to that chakra. This section in each chapter will share challenges that indicate that this chakra's energy is closed for you.
If Open:	When a chakra's energy is active, strong, and balanced, it influences your life in a positive way. This section in each chapter will share positive manifestations of this energy in your life when the chakra is open and activated.
Affirmation:	In each chapter, you will find an affirmation specific to each chakra. It is a declaration you can repeat to empower and activate the function of the chakra.
Carol Tuttle Healing Oil Blend:	You can use physical resources to help your energetic system adapt to the new energy of our times. I recommend a custom essential oil blend for each chakra to support your system in our modern-day experience.

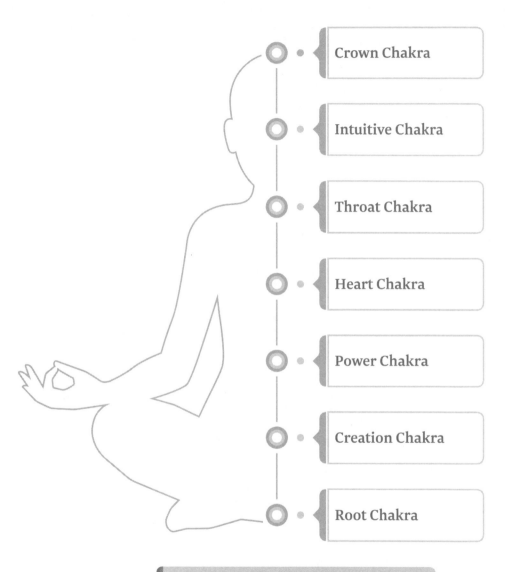

Crown Chakra

Intuitive Chakra

Throat Chakra

Heart Chakra

Power Chakra

Creation Chakra

Root Chakra

Foot Chakra

I have a strong attraction energy that supports me
in creating what is correct and timely for me.

Before You Step, Take a Stand!

. . . .

Chakra 0—The Foot Chakra

Location:	Below the feet
Yin/Yang Flow:	None
Universal Color:	None
Associated Organs and Body Parts:	Feet and lower legs. Imbalances in this chakra can create issues with your feet and lower legs.
Function:	The magnetic plate creating an attractor field. First floor of the root chakra, connected to taking a stand.
Old Energy:	I stand together with the collective energy of my family or culture.
New Energy	I am standing in my unique truth as a powerful individual and am connected to my unique life path and purpose.
If Closed:	Manifesting what you want in your life is difficult. You have trouble staying focused and accomplishing things. You feel as if you never move forward or progress at the rate you know you are capable of.
If Open:	You are able to manifest and attract to you what is timely and supportive. You feel you have a unique place on the planet and stand in your own truth. You get things done in a timely and efficient manner.
Affirmation:	I am taking my unique place on the planet. I have a strong attraction energy that supports me in creating what is correct and timely for me.
Carol Tuttle Healing Oil Blends:	I am connected I am grounded

Before you can take your first step to awakening, you have to choose to stand. Taking a stand for your truth is supported energetically by the foot chakra. The foot chakra energy is a plate of energy that is your unique place to stand.

You have probably heard the term "personal space," which refers to the energetic container or energy bubble that surrounds your body. Or you may be familiar with what an auric field is. The foot chakra is similar, in that it is a personal energy field. Its energy presents as though you are standing in an energetic plate (or field—depending on how large yours is), and it moves with you, just as your aura moves as a constant energy around you. This field creates a point of attraction for you to manifest what is desired, timely, and correct for you. I started to notice this chakra around 2004 as an energy that was presenting itself in people's energy fields. Using my intuitive gift of tuning into this energy, I could see the history of this energy being birthed into our modern-day experience.

THE OLD ENERGY OF THE FOOT CHAKRA
In the chapters that follow, I will share the Old Energy of each chakra—in other words, the way each chakra's energy influenced people's lives prior to 1960. But the individual foot chakra is the only one that I cannot write much about the Old Energy, as this chakra energy was not activated on an individual level before the 1950s and 60s.

The foot chakra is associated with taking a stand. People have been taking a stand for centuries, but before the birth of the individual foot chakra, they always did so with a collective energy. In the Old Energy of the foot chakra, people were all held energetically on plates of energy that were tribal in their effect. We were connected to our familial energy system, and also our given societies' energy fields. Groups with common beliefs or common goals came together to make change. But people who tried to take an individual stand, completely against or independent from of a group or system, were most likely to be killed or shut down.

When the foot chakra started to become activated in our personal (rather than collective) energy systems, a shift occurred in humanity. Instead of being energetically bound by the tribal energy field and leaders of the tribe, we were birthed into having our own independent stand on what we believe is correct and good for the whole. This new energy supported people in thinking independently and taking a stand for what they believed was correct, even if it countered the collective energy of family, religion, or society.

THE NEW ENERGY OF THE FOOT CHAKRA

The individual foot chakra is a new energy that started birthing itself in our energy field in the mid to late 1950s. It is connected to the idea of taking a stand as an individual experience of expression, rather than taking a stand as a group of people. We can see this in many places in the world. I will share examples from the history of the United States, which is where I live. But you can find evidence of this new energy having an effect on the thinking and choices that started to present in society all over the world since that time.

Some of the clearest examples of this new energy started in the 1950s, with some front runners of humanity like Rosa Parks. On December 1, 1955, Parks refused to give up her seat to a white passenger and "took a stand" to resist racial segregation.[20] Even though her action is now seen as part of a larger civil rights movement, Rosa's decision was made and acted on alone. In that moment, she made a choice that was different from what anyone in that situation had done before. She didn't do it with a group of people. Rosa herself made the choice and took an individual stand.

Following those years, the way the foot chakra influenced people's views, values, and choices is evident in the uprising of independent thought and action that was so prevalent in the 1960s. I had the blessing of growing up as a child of the '60s. I lived in an area in the United States where many changes in American culture took place. Growing up in the suburbs of San Francisco and Berkley California, I not only had a close-up view of what was happening, but I was also part of the bigger energy shift going on at that time. Just a few of the events of the '60s show that the foot chakra was activating in our individual energy fields, including the women's rights movement, civil rights movement, and the birth of rock music. It was a decade of people taking a stand for injustice.

Taking a stand has happened in many ways throughout history, but prior to the 1960s, it happened in a more collective way. For example, the United States itself was founded by people taking a stand, but it was done so by a group. For almost 200 years after that, the collective body of energy in the United States deemed war as patriotic, whether it was on different collective sides in the American Civil War, or much later during World Wars I and II that united the country. If you took a stand against war, you were considered anti-American and risked the chance of being arrested or at least seen as a traitor to your country.

The New Energy of the foot chakra—activated in the 1950s and 1960s—manifested as an individual experience of taking a stand. As this energy was activated, anti-war protests became prevalent for the first time in American history. People were no longer willing to be blindly led by tribal or government leaders. They were willing to "take a stand" in greater numbers than American culture had ever seen, for what they individually felt was correct. We could say that the practice of "taking a stand" was born with the presenting energy of the foot chakra.

MODERN EXAMPLES OF FOOT CHAKRA ENERGY IN TAKING A STAND

At the time of writing this book, the #MeToo movement took off. This movement encouraged women to stand up and tell the truth regarding any sexual assault or sexual harassment they had experienced in their life. (As you will read later in the 2nd chakra section, the energy of the 2nd chakra is all about owning our sexuality and having a choice with it. The #MeToo movement is an example of women taking a stand to enforce that as the new norm.) Many famous men were "called out" publicly for sexual harassment and sexual assault. As a result, they lost their credibility, and in many cases, their jobs. They were not legally made accountable, yet they were made morally accountable by their social falling out in the public eye. Women's marches became a regular occurrence in many metropolitan cities.

At that time, a new Justice of the Supreme Court was being selected in the United States. During the review process to determine if Brett Kavanaugh was worthy and qualified for a Supreme Court position, a woman named Christine Blasey Ford came forward with allegations of sexual assault from when she and Kavanaugh attended high school together.[21] The story kicked off hot debate, with people strongly taking sides about what they denied or believed to be true about the allegations. In the days following, many women who were personally victims of sexual assault and harassment became vocal online and in person about this story, protesting and speaking out in outrage against anyone who did not believe Kavanaugh was guilty.

I share this story, not to weigh in on the allegations or the individuals involved, but purely to show the power of the "taking a stand" energy in our modern-day culture. As I observed the energetics feeding into this cultural occurrence, it became clear to me that the theme of the energy was taking a stand for injustice. Injustices should be accounted for. If they aren't, the energy shows up somewhere else. Many of the women who felt invested in Kavanaugh's case never had anyone take a stand for their own injustices. Their desire for someone to stand up and make someone accountable for their misdeeds and assaults led them to have stronger reactions to Kavanaugh's case than they might have had otherwise. They felt the emotion of their own experience play out in the hearing, and felt personally invested because the energy had never been accounted for. I was a victim of sexual assault myself, and so I understand the primal yearning for someone to be accountable for their horrific actions. Somebody needed to account for the misdeeds of men towards women and Kavanaugh became the national symbol of that need. As I watched this event play out energetically, I saw the energy of taking a stand for injustice get called up and directed at one person, regardless of whether he was guilty or not.

Again, I do not share this story to discuss the actual details of the hearing itself, but the energetic reaction surrounding it. This is purely my observation of the power of the foot chakra energy becoming stronger and stronger since it was first birthed in the 1950s and 60s. As this energy comes alive in our energy fields, it feeds into the larger cultural story we are creating as humans. We will continue to take a stand as a society against injustices that were not stood up for in the past. It is important for us to take a stand and make sure the energy is accounted for on an individual level, so that more public events do not become overwhelming or distressing to so many people. We are supported with a new energy that empowers us to take those stands. The energy of our time is instant karma! We are being held accountable to our choices with very short turnarounds.

This New Energy is being manifest in locations throughout the world, not just the United States. One of the most well-known modern examples is Malala Yousafzai, who took an individual stand by pursuing her education in a region of the world where others were willing to try and stop her violently. It was risky enough that she was actually shot by a gunman. But she didn't let that stop her. Because Malala took a stand, she has created a shift large enough for others to also be empowered in pursuing what is correct for them.[22] How do we feed the energy of taking a stand for what is right so that we all receive the benefit of standing in our truth and being supported? By taking a stand for our children when it is appropriate. By taking a stand for our own inner child and creating a space for healing.

What is asking you to take a stand in your life right now? As you identify what you're meant to take a stand on, your personal choice to feed this energy in your day-to-day life will help all of us get to a place where good choices are made more frequently. As we each take a stand for the good, we birth the energy of goodwill and raise children who will create that world of all people standing in their truth and being honored and respected for it.

HOW IMPORTANT IS IT TO STAND IN YOUR TRUTH?

I have been asked if the commotion and craziness of this time in the world will ever quiet down. I say that all depends on what you choose. It depends on the truth you choose to stand in. Even though the world is full of a lot of noise and controversy, I don't live a loud and crazy life. The purpose of standing in your truth is not about making the outer world settle down. You create the calm in your own sphere of day-to-day reality.

Being rooted to the earth's energy supports you in standing in your truth. If no one took a stand for you in your childhood, you may either find it challenging to take a stand for yourself and your children, or you may go to extremes in taking a stand. You can practice taking a stand for yourself in a way that is healthy with the exercises at the end of this chapter.

You can also strengthen this new energy for the next generation by taking a stand for the children in your life. This brief story illustrates how simple but powerful that experience can be. An online follower of my work shared the story of her six-year-old son going through shameful experiences at school, due to his teacher's disciplinary style. The teacher had unreasonable expectations for how well children could focus and sit still while learning. The child in this experience was a higher movement—The Fun-Loving Type 1 Child, as I teach in my book *The Child Whisperer*. As the mother described:

> *"The things I've seen [the teacher] do seem shaming, and rude to me. She will take pencils away from her students and erase their work if she doesn't feel it is good enough, and make them do it again. If the child doesn't do their homework they now have to use their recess time doing homework. If a child is moving, they are told they have to sit completely still and follow her directions exactly… I just don't like how she singles students out, especially in front of everyone."*

This mother went on to share that she didn't feel she had any power to change the situation for her son and thought she could possibly make up the difference in his home environment. I replied:

*"Why do you think you have no power to change what is
happening to him at school? You absolutely have power and the
right as his parent to not settle for this and either have changes
made in the classroom or change teachers. Your efforts at home
will not make up the difference for what is happening at school."*

She answered:

*"I don't know. I have never liked confrontation, and I almost
always feel bad after I have confronted someone. It very well
could be because of how my parents responded whenever I would
tell them I was unhappy, or how they made me feel. They were
always very quick to point out what I was doing wrong, and
do everything they could to make me feel guilty. I find myself
standing up to people more since I've had children, and other
times wishing I'd stood up for my kiddos. I guess I am unsure how
to approach this situation."*

I encouraged this mom to take a stand for her son and either talk
to the teacher or the principal to help effect a change. This mom took
what I shared to heart and decided she could talk to the teacher, free
of conflict or confrontation. Because she believed she could speak up
about this and that she would be supported, the outcome was favorable.
The teacher received her feedback well and they are now working in a
cooperative way to help her son have a more positive experience in the
classroom.

Notice that the woman's fear of speaking up for her child went all the way back to her own childhood. This situation was setting her up to resolve that old energy and activate the new energy of taking a stand. Consider the possibility that something is showing up in your life with the primary purpose of being a "set-up" to support you in having the experience of taking a stand for yourself or someone or something in your life. Decide now that you can take that stand in a way that not only honors yourself but also others involved. Trust that your act of taking a stand will shift the experience to create a favorable outcome.

Exercises to Strengthen the New Energy of the Foot Chakra

Use any and all of the following exercises to help you ground the new energy of the foot chakra into your personal energy system. You can use them as frequently as you find supportive.

Energy Circles

Energy circles are a powerful creation technique to help you ground your desires, positive thoughts, and affirmations to your foot chakra, which will help bring them in to material form in your life.

1. Stand up and ground yourself by focusing on your feet and the surface beneath your feet.

2. Think of 10 things you desire to bring into material manifestation. What do you really want? (If 10 seems like too many, consider the possibility that you have room to expand in what you believe you're able to create.)

3. Write out your desires as affirmations using "I am" statements. Here are some general examples:
   - I am successful
   - I am living my true purpose
   - I am financially successful
   - I am healthy and happy
   - I am grateful for my beautiful relationships

4. Stand up, bend over, and draw a circle on the ground with your hand, as far out as you can reach around your feet. Actually touch the floor to draw the circle. (This is the space of your foot chakra.)

5. Imagine the circle lighting up under your feet. State the "I am" statements you wrote down. As you do, make the motion of throwing them into the circle with your hand.

6. Bend over and gather up the energy in your hands. Bring this energy up from your foot chakra into yourself by massaging the energy into your body, starting at your feet, as if you're painting your body with the energy.

7. Gather up the energy again with your hand and throw your hands to the heavens, inviting your spirit guides and highest self to help you create your desires.

8. Place your hands on your heart chakra (center of your chest) as you express gratitude for the opportunity to be a creator of your life.

Walking Barefoot in the Grass or Dirt

When the weather permits, walk in the grass or dirt for several minutes and feel the life force energy of the earth moving up your feet.

Looking at Your Feet While You Are Walking

Where you place your attention, more energy goes. By looking at your feet while you walk for several minutes, you flow energy into your foot chakra. Think about what you want to create along your life path as you walk.

Gardening

Spending time gardening reinforces the creation process of planting seeds, nurturing them to grow, and bearing the fruits of the what the seeds grow. The act of gardening represents the energy and objective of the foot chakra, which is to support you in manifesting your desires.

Taking a Healthy Stand for Something You Believe In and Helping It Progress

Take a stand for a project, person, cause, goal, or idea that you believe in. This practice can be as simple as taking a stand for better health, a happy life, financial success—anything that you are determined to change in your life. It can also look like taking a stand for someone in your life by showing up for them, or a movement or cause you believe in by getting more involved with it.

Grounding Yourself with Essential Oils

A nurturing foot massage activates the energies of your feet and helps you feel more grounded and connected to the earth. Carol Tuttle Healing Oils are custom blends that support you with specific healing goals. These oil blends can be used to activate and strengthen this chakra in the following ways:

- **I am grounded:** This oil assists you in connecting with your own body and the energy of the earth. Using this oil serves as a reminder that you have have a right to be here and a purpose in which to contribute your gifts. This oil also provides a unique benefit of clearing your personal energy system of the side effects of excessive exposure to EMF (Electro Magnetic Frequencies) that are emitted from cell phones and computers.
- **I am balanced:** This oil blend assists you in activating, strengthening, and balancing the entire chakra system. It can be used on any individual chakra, or be applied to all 7 chakras to activate and strengthen the entire system. As a result, you will experience more harmony and balance as you take you stand.

What key thing did you learn from this section?

Use this space to make notes. Write down questions and insights you had while reading this section.

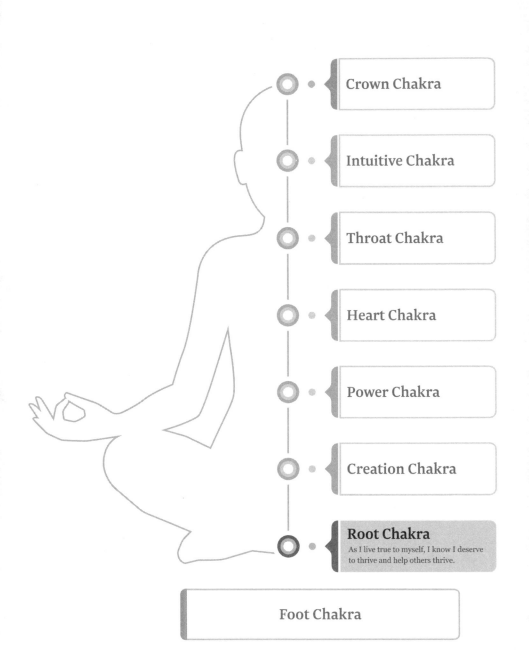

Crown Chakra

Intuitive Chakra

Throat Chakra

Heart Chakra

Power Chakra

Creation Chakra

Root Chakra
As I live true to myself, I know I deserve
to thrive and help others thrive.

Foot Chakra

Step 1: Claiming Your Roots

· · · · · · ·

1st Chakra—The Root Chakra

Location:	Underneath the torso in the area of the perineum.
Yin/Yang Flow:	Both yang moving down into the earth, then yin as life force energy from the earth moves up and into us.
Universal Color:	Red
Associated Organs and Body Parts:	Legs, hips, immune system. Imbalance in this chakra can manifest physically as issues with constipation, weight, or fatigue.
Function:	Energetically connecting us to the earth and our life path and purpose.
Old Energy:	I have to deny my true self and help the tribe survive.
New Energy	I am finding and living true to myself so I can then use my gifts and talents to help the tribe thrive.
If Closed:	You struggle with putting others first and not making your needs and wants a priority. You think you have to fix others' problems. You struggle with financial debt and lack of money, poor health, and physical illness. You carry an underlying sense of not being worth it and not belonging.
If Open:	You flow and accumulate plenty of money, you enjoy a healthy body, you feel like you belong. You have a strong connection with family and/or friends while living true to yourself, using your gifts and talents to make a difference in the world.
Affirmation:	As I live true to myself, I know I deserve to thrive and help others thrive.
Carol Tuttle Healing Oil Blends:	I am connected I am healthy

The first step in awakening starts with the root chakra—being rooted or grounded in your own truth. The root chakra energy connects us with the earth. The energy of the root chakra is in the pelvic area of your torso and the area of your lower groin. All life begins here as an infant enters the world through the pelvic floor, in the energetic space of the root chakra. Root chakra energy moves down your legs and feet, connecting to the foot chakra.

When root chakra energy is healthy, rooted, and thriving, we feel we are a part of humanity, while still maintaining an independent sense of self. We hold our own energy and experience our own emotion. We feel clear on our personal values with a strong sense of standing in our own truth. Our primary physical needs are met. In today's modern era, that means we have a healthy flow and accumulation of money and a mindful approach to using money as a tool to invest in our needs and wants. We feel that life supports us and that we will always have our needs and wants met. We are on a path moving forward with a purpose to our life. We are our own person and we maintain our energetic autonomy in all our relationships. We can say, "I am my own person and I know where I stand on what is important to me. Life supports me and all my needs and wants are met."

If you are not rooted to your own truth, you will find it challenging to move forward on your life path and feel that you have a distinct purpose beyond the roles you play or the work you do to pay the bills. Without being rooted, life becomes monotonous, as you are not grounded to a sense of identity or a unique purpose to play.

THE OLD ENERGY OF THE ROOT CHAKRA

The old energy of the root chakra has been an energetic connection in sub groups and larger cultural groups. In years past, this first energy center has been rooted in the energy of our tribal ancestors, with the focus on what will help the family survive.

Look back into our ancestors' experience with the root chakra energy. The family they were born into was their main energetic connection to the world. They were part of a family energy system that was energetically connected to the earth. They were not energetically independent of their family, and being part of this larger energy system influenced who they were (or were not) supposed to be in their lifetime.

Personal energy melded with the family's energy system. They were one and the same. People did not have energetic autonomy from their family. They were inclined to make choices based on values that were energetically influenced by the family system. They existed to please their family and parents' values, making decisions from the perspective of how it would affect the family and fulfill expectations. The focus was not on the self, but rather the family unit first.

As we became a more modern society, this conformity to the group energy had a certain pattern. For men, it often looked like growing up and either going to college or getting a job, in order to work and provide an income for their family. For women, this pattern looked like staying home and raising children. Roles were defined without reference to the self or individual needs, preferences, or situations.

The old energy of the root chakra has influenced the experience of physical survival on the planet. This included feeling safe in the world and having basic needs met. In today's world, this sense of safety translates into enough money and physical health. The old energy was more primal and focused on survival because survival was the experience.

In more modern times, far fewer people have to concern themselves on a daily basis with just surviving. Yet, until you consciously choose to activate the new energy of the root chakra in your system, you will create patterns of struggle and survival repeatedly with money and your physical health.

Most teachers of the chakra energy system would tell you that the energy of money is in the root chakra, as it is a basic need in our modern times. I used to teach this as well. But at the turn of the century, I had an experience with the energy of money. (When you are an intuitive empath, anything can speak to you!) The energy of money told me it was being upgraded to the heart chakra. As the chakra energy shifts, we are shifting from surviving to thriving, and this includes our experience with money.

The lower three chakras relate to all things in the physical world—what has form and substance. Money used to be a commodity that we physically interacted with. However, in our digital era, we no longer have our primary experience with money as a tangible, physical one. It is electronic. And the energy of the chakras has shifted money to a higher calling. In the past, money has been used as a form of power and control by the few who had large sums to control the majority. With money being more and more of an even playing field, it has been moved to the heart energy to allow us to use the tool of money to serve and make a difference on the planet. Some of the forerunners of this energetic shift have created stories with money that have helped us all receive the benefit of this shift. One example is Bill and Melinda Gates. Two of the wealthiest people on the planet have chosen to use their money to make a difference. Money is a powerful tool that I will teach you more about in the heart chakra section. In that section, I will help you upgrade your money energy to the heart, so you can "do what you love and the money will follow!"

THE NEW ENERGY OF THE ROOT CHAKRA

The entire root energy system is comprised of the bottom of your torso, your legs, and feet, which connect to your energy plate in the earth that moves with you wherever you go. The energetic shift that is taking place in the root chakra is actually causing the patterns of the old energy to be uprooted. You may have felt this shift personally. The following are indicators that the new energy of the 1st chakra is getting activated for you and you are being "uprooted" from the old family system energy. How many of these have you experienced?

- You feel a lack of clarity about who you are and what you want in life.
- You struggle with maintaining your own energetic autonomy around certain people and find yourself catering to them, pleasing them, and putting yourself second.
- You struggle with money and have fear and anxiety around not having enough.
- You don't believe you can have what you want. You are still going without and telling yourself it's not that bad.
- When you are with your extended family, you seem to turn into a completely different person.
- You notice that you know how everyone else is feeling and you have no idea how *you* feel in many situations.
- You feel confused on where you stand with your values and what's important to you.
- You take on other people's energy.

- Because you do a lot of the above, you pay a price physically, which means you are constantly dealing with sickness, ill health, or weight issues.
- You still believe life is a struggle.

Based on how you identified with the above scenarios, you can see that you are experiencing a shift just like the rest of the planet! It's not just you; we are all going through this process of awakening.

We have been energetically rooted for centuries in the energy of the collective. With the continuing collapse of cultural hierarchy and the belief that a power outside of ourselves will take care of us, we have been uprooted from generations of our ancestors' energetic roots. Because of this energetic shift, we are free to be rooted to our own energy, to claim from our ancestors the energetic patterns that support and serve us, and to let go of the ones that do not.

Ask yourself: Who am I? What do I want for me and my family? What do I value? What do I stand for? Which values and principles do I want to pass on to my children?

LOOKING AT YOUR ANCESTORS' ENERGETIC ROOTS

I have had the opportunity to do family genealogy for both my mother's and father's ancestral lines. I have been able to trace my mother's direct family line back to 1585 and learn some of their stories and their history. My 13th great-grandfather was a ship builder who came from England to start a shipyard in the area that is now the coast of Delaware. From this story, I know that I have builder energy in my roots. My grandfather owned Tull Hardware, a successful hardware store in New England. From this story, I know I have tools in my roots. My own career reflects this energy that has influenced my own path in life. I am the author of numerous books that help people rebuild their lives from struggle to joy, and I teach people new tools that they can use to do this in my books and online courses.

On my father's side, I have traced my ancestry back six generations and learned some of their stories that I carry the energy of in my roots. My great-grandfather and his brother were successful beer brewers on the East Coast. They had a thriving business. When prohibition was instated in the United States, legislation made selling and buying alcohol illegal. It destroyed my ancestors' successful business. Their business dissolved. My grandfather hit some very hard times economically. His brother went on to be one of the first to invent low-alcohol-content beer to comply with prohibition requirements. He started a new business venture, but did not include my great-grandfather. My great uncle went on to make a fortune and my great-grandfather never financially recovered. He died a poor man with many physical problems. He resented his brother and felt he had been stabbed in the back, as he had been the one to bring his brother into the brewing business in the first place. He looked out for his brother, but his brother did not do the same for him.

From this story, I learn that I carry many energetic impressions in my root energy, both positive and negative. Let's look at the negative patterns that I have had a chance to clear. Seeing this process can help you also start to recognize old family patterns that influence your root chakra.

My great-grandfather died with resentment and anger, and as a result the pattern in our family system passed on to my father. My dad first tipped me off to this pattern when I would hear him say, "You have to be careful or someone is going to stab you in the back." My dad was a successful entrepreneur and he did create a few "back-stabbing" bad deals in his business career. As I put two and two together, I realized that my father carried the energy of resentment and anger that can come from being stabbed in the back by bad business deals. Is it possible that in earlier times that I have an ancestor that could have literally been stabbed in the back and either killed or wounded? Very much so! I have not traced that ancestral line back past the early 1800s to know and there are no records within our family of any such story. I just know that energy presented itself, based on my great-grandfather's experience and my dad's. The language my father used gave me an opportunity to recognize that energy and clear it from my roots.

Take a moment and reflect on what you know about your ancestors and their life stories. Which energetic roots from those stories may you still be connected to that you can now uproot from? What energetic roots from their stories do you want to help influence your life for the good?

If you don't have much (or any) information about your ancestors' lives, look around your own life. Notice the patterns that seem to come up over and over, even when you try to do something different. I can almost guarantee that those energetic patterns were handed down to you from generations before, even if you don't know the story behind them.

Which of your ancestors' energetic roots are you ready to clear? Which of your ancestors' energetic roots are you hoping to grow deeper and stronger?

MODERN FAMILY ENERGY ARCHETYPES— WHICH ROLE DO YOU PLAY?

In today's world, we tend to play out energetic archetypes in our family systems that keep everybody stuck in lower states of consciousness. These archetypes are held in the root chakra, as that is the energy center where we are rooted to our family. When you take your first step in awakening to your truth, you are choosing to step into your own energy and free yourself of your family of origin's dysfunctional energy. That may look like literally walking away, or it can be more of an energetic stance that you take while interacting with your family. Only you can know what is correct for you.

An energy archetype is an energetic pattern that has been created over decades of people choosing into roles. The energy can be so powerful that it functions like deeply held roots in our family system, influencing how we think, perceive our world, and behave in our family experience.

Waking up from old family roles you play is a practice in uprooting yourself from your family's energy to grow the roots of your own energy and truth. Which of these energy archetypes are you ready to uproot yourself from?

The Victim

The victim child carries the energy of powerlessness for the family. They feel powerless and angry for not being given the support that they need. They complain frequently about other family members and how Mom and Dad have let them down. They feel little need to change, as their victim status provides them a sense of entitlement. They subconsciously hope the entitlement they feel they deserve will be materialized someday. Other family members complain about the victim and judge them with comments like, "When are they ever going to get it? They are such a baby about things. Why don't they do something about it rather than complain?" If you are not the victim child it is easy to project your judgment onto that person and have a superior attitude about yourself. In comparison, your life may look a lot better, which keeps you from self-accountability and doing your own personal healing work. In my Energy Profiling system, all 4 Energy Types can be prone to playing the victim role.

The Rebel

The rebel child carries anger for the family system. They are angry at Mom and Dad for letting them down. They are angry they have to conform to the family's societal views, and they are angry that they did not have their needs met. As they carry others' anger, they could be running Mom and Dad's anger or other siblings' anger. This allows them to be ostracized from the family and for other family members to project onto them that they need to get over their anger. What the other family members don't realize is that this family member is actually carrying the anger for multiple family members, as others are not taking accountability for what they are angry about. The rebel archetype allows family members who are not taking responsibility for their anger to point fingers and say, "Look at them. They are so angry. That is wrong and selfish. All they think about is themselves." If they understood the rebel child is running the anger for everyone they might say, "Look at them. They are doing us all a favor. I really need to own my anger so they don't have to do it for me." If you are a rebel child, I encourage you to give back the anger to everyone in your family! Let them work out what they are angry about. In my Energy Profiling system, Type 3 and Type 4 people are more likely to play the role of the rebel child.

The Pleaser

The pleaser child is trying to help the family get along and smooth out the energy. They forego taking care of their own needs so often that they forget how, or never even learn how, as this role is taken on early in childhood. They are always looking outside themselves to see how everyone else is doing. They become the intersection of everyone's dysfunctional energy by playing the mediator, even into their adult lives. Family members call or text them about the issues they are having with other family members. They try to accommodate everyone and make everyone happy. They sacrifice their own well-being on behalf of everyone else. They subconsciously learn that their value comes from playing this role. It is not sustainable, as our true value is something we connect with deep down, not something we create from playing a role. In my Energy Profiling system, it is more common for Type 1 and Type 2 people to take on the role of the pleaser child.

The Good Child

The good child carries the energy of trying to get their needs met by doing what they perceive their parents want. This can be a version of the pleaser child; the biggest difference is that this child will compare themselves to other siblings who are not as "good" and deem themselves more lovable. This archetypal energy was created more recently in our modern-day era, where our doings gained so much attention and recognition. This role can also shift very suddenly from being the good child to being the rebel child in an effort to get out of the energetic hold. The challenge is, rebel energy is a countermove that creates a false sense of independence, but is really still captured by the family energy system. In my Energy Profiling system, any Type can play the role of the good child.

The Sick One

The sick child learns to get value and their needs met from being sick. When there is not enough unconditional love from Mom and Dad to go around, a child learns that illness can give you more attention and a chance to be noticed. You can carry this pattern into your adult life and still get sick as a pattern. If you took on the belief, "I have to be sick to get my needs met," when you were five and you have never altered that pattern, it is still operating in you and causing you to stay sick and ill.

In my Energy Profiling System, any Type can take on the role of the sick child, but it tends to be more common for Type 2 people.

The Estranged One

The estranged child takes on the energy of the broken family system. It is so strongly held by this child, they have to separate themselves in order to feel they can survive their life. Not every family system runs this archetypal energy. For those that do, it can be a pattern that continues for generations. My family of origin had this archetypal energy that went back five generations. My father estranged himself from his parents by moving across the country and barely talking to them after the move. I estranged myself from my family of origin for five years. I have cleared that energy so it will no longer play out in my family. In my case, abuse of many forms, including physical, sexual, and emotional went back five generations and had never been healed. I took on the energy of abuse for my family so strongly that my PTSD would get triggered with any contact with my family members. When a family member takes on an issue that is so deeply wounding, and nobody in the family system is willing to talk about it, the estranged child has to move away to keep their sanity. I distinctly remember that my choice to estrange myself from my family was for personal survival and the survival of my adult family that I had created. In my Energy Profiling system, any Type can take on this role, but as always, they will move through the experience in their own way.

The Black Sheep Child

There are many forms of the black sheep child. You could be the black sheep from playing the role of the rebel child, the sick child, or the estranged child. Either way, you don't feel like you fit into your family system as easily as the rest of the group. For most black sheep, this role is created by the experience of having a different energetic configuration than your other family members. You have a different operating system. It's like being an Apple computer and your family members are all PC computers—you just have different programming. Neither is better, they are just different. The challenge is, when you are little, you may interpret the differences you feel as evidence that you are less valuable and not as lovable. You couldn't rationalize why you felt different; you just knew you did. It is important that you don't make your difference into a story and create more drama from it. You *are* different. But you can learn to connect and be part of your family in your own way. Self-confidence is the foundation that will support you in doing this. Being rooted in your own truth stabilizes you to connect with people of all energetic varieties, including your family. In my Energy Profiling system, any person can feel like the black sheep. The big factor is the Energy Types of other family members.

ARE YOU STILL ROOTED IN YOUR FAMILY OF ORIGIN'S DYSFUNCTIONAL ENERGY PATTERNS?

Some people believe they are independent of their family-of-origin energy, yet they are not. They are rebelling against it or trying to fix it, rather than just having family relationships while staying free of the family dysfunction.

How do you know if you're still stuck in that energy? You can ask yourself a few questions: Do I feel or sense judgment from my family that bothers me? Do I ever feel stuck or unable to act because of how another family member will probably respond? Do I sometimes feel family members are yanking my chain, trying to get me to play old roles in my family system? Which of the energy archetypes do I fall into when I am around my family of origin?

Here's a story that will help you see how simply and powerfully you can release those old patterns and root your own energy in family relationships. Sam is a 31-year-old male who comes from a family of three sisters and parents who have been unhappily married for most of their 32-year marriage. Sam has partially removed himself from creating drama and struggle with the family members, but not entirely. He no longer creates upsetting experiences with any of his family members directly. But he is still involved by being willing to be the sounding board or mediator of the drama that they create with each other. A recent conversation he was having with his mother went like this:

Mom: *Your father is just mean. He's just rude to me. He tries to listen to what I want to change until he can't anymore and just puts it back on me.*

Sam: *Mom, he's hurting just as much as you are. His intentions are good, he wants to be with you, he cares about you.*

Mom: *Well I am just tired. I don't know if I should stay with him any longer.*

Sam's mom has been saying the same thing since he was 12 years old. One night when he was 12, she tucked him in bed and asked him, "Sam, should I stay with your father?" In that moment 12-year-old Sam was enrolled in the job of mediating his parents' miserable marriage. No child wants their parents to divorce and he felt a weight of responsibility to keep them from doing so.

I had Sam do a visualization with his 12-year-old self and hand that job back to his mom and dad. He broke down in tears, as he had been carrying that energy from his parents for 19 years! He set his 12-year-old self free that day and gave the energy of his parents' dysfunctional marriage back to them, so he no longer had to carry it on his path.

What are you carrying for your family that isn't yours to carry? When you are energetically your own person, standing in your own truth and light, you no longer feel the need to react against your family or try to fix it. You are no longer triggered by your family members' choices. You no longer speak ill of family and you no longer have any desire to be a part of the old energy of family struggle and drama with them in any way.

So how do you have a relationship with your family when they are still operating in dysfunctional energy patterns? It takes time to establish a different role and rapport with your family, but with practice you can achieve it. You have to gain stamina to hold your own so that they do not trigger you. You can let them know you are not interested in getting involved in their life issues and you trust they will find answers to their challenges. Interact with them by listening, validating them, loving them and making suggestions to do fun and enjoyable activities together. You may find you spend less time with them, yet the time you do spend is pleasant and enjoyable for everyone. You can become the family member that everyone feels loved and supported by.

How do you know when you are energetically free from your family system energy? You no longer judge it or are emotionally triggered by it. You can observe it and appreciate it for what it is—an experience that many people are choosing to have.

ARE YOU STILL ROOTED TO A PARENT'S ENERGY?

Instead of your entire family of origin, your energy may be rooted to one or both of your parents. Connection with a loving parent is good, but being energetically rooted to them can leave you compromised. The following story will show you how that can play out, and give you insight into what to do about it. This story comes from a client of my online resource, The Carol Tuttle Healing Center. Every year at the time of her father's passing, this woman went into deep grief that was disabling and painful for her to revisit. She shared these words in the private group for Healing Center Members:

> *"My dad passed away 5 years ago this month and I seem to relive feeling a very deep grief from his passing each year and I feel lost without him here."*

> *I tuned into her energy, and I could see the issue keeping her from healing, so I shared the following with her:*

> *"In the chakra energy system you have a root chakra. This energy connects your personal energy system to the planet. I sense your personal energy system was rooted through your dad's root chakra. Since he is not here, you have been uprooted and need to create your own personal energetic root system. The work you are doing in the Healing Center is assisting you with this. I would add to your energy circles statements such as:*

> *—I am now rooted in my own life*
> *—I am connected to my father spiritually now (the upper chakras are where this connection occurs)*

—*I am standing on my own with my own root system*
—*I am strong*

Several weeks later, she followed up with her progress sharing this:

"The big thing that Carol hit on that I needed was that I could receive my dad's support in a spiritual presence much more than hanging onto any earthly experiences with him. I 100% know my dad is still with me. I never would have thought I really believed in that until he passed, but some really crazy things have happened and I just know it was him.

Carol also mentioned that I should think about unraveling the earthly attachments I might still have to him from around age 7-8. When she said that, I knew why this time of year was most difficult for me. He did pass on December 16th, but it's really Christmas. My childhood memories of him are all about Christmas. He dressed up and came to school and played Christmas carols for my classes on his guitar, he hid presents all around the house with scavenger hunts, he carefully changed "Noel" on wrapping paper to "Noelle" with a gold sharpie.

My dad and I were always close. He believed in everything I did and supported me 100% through everything. I have definitely felt lost at times without him. So, I'm acknowledging all of those feelings. My plan now is to work on a few things (1) fear of being here without him, (2) guilt that we didn't do more when he was sick, (3) letting go of resentment that he's gone, and (4) the deeper feelings of needing him that are disabling to me."

As you read that, what thought came up about your own experience? Your root chakra energy may be intertwined with a living or deceased parent. This can happen whether you had a healthy or unhealthy relationship with this parent.

Take a moment to close your eyes and imagine you can look at the roots that are growing beneath your feet. Are your roots tight and bound with a parent's root energy? Do you see that the roots are choking and constricted as you continue to play out patterns of being your parent's pleaser or victim? Take a moment and imagine you can unbind the roots and pull the energy of your parents' roots out of yours. Follow up with the plugging-in exercise and other root chakra exercises taught at the end of this chapter.

ARE YOU UPROOTING FROM YOUR FAMILY'S DYSFUNCTIONAL ENERGY?

Look back at your life path and consider which decisions you made or life experiences you had that helped you uproot from the energy of your family of origin. Some of these decisions may have been painful and severed family ties; others were easy choices that supported you along the way in becoming your own person. They all helped put you on your own path of learning the lesson of standing in your own truth.

I made the first decision that began my uprooting process was when I was 18. I graduated from high school and four days later, I drove with my brother from California to Utah to start my freshman year of college during summer term. Once I moved out, I only went back one summer to live at home and work. I can see now that getting out on my own, independent of my family and my parents' energetic influence supported me in growing my own roots of self-identity.

The second significant phase of my uprooting from my family energy system occurred when I was 30. At the time, my husband worked for my father, my parents lived 15 minutes away from us, I had daily contact with my mother, and my husband had daily contact with my father. My father had learned of my choice to heal my abusive background and he was actively playing out a role as a dysfunctional perpetrator by putting the blame on me and my "craziness." He was persistent in trying to shut me down, which added repeated abuse and trauma to my life. I was in the depths of depression and PTSD.

With the lack of healing resources available to me at that time in my life, I felt strongly impressed as an answer to prayer that my husband and I were to move out of the state where we lived and start a new life elsewhere. I knew that in order to heal, I had to relocate and get out on my own. I could not be so deeply immersed in my family's dysfunctional culture and energy and expect healing to occur and last. This move led me to choosing not to have any contact with my father. My choice to not have contact with my father led to my mother choosing not to have contact with me. This makes sense to me. My father's aggressive behavior would have made it very hard for her to take a stand for me, when she had not healed her own emotional wounds. My siblings followed suit and I went five years being estranged from my family.

As I look back now, I understand how this move helped me take a stand for myself and create my own energetic roots of truth. It was difficult and painful and I don't recommend anyone follow in my footsteps unless they feel the hand of God moving them in that direction.

Five years after we moved, I was strongly impressed upon to reach out to my family and renew those relationships, moving forward, looking at our future together, and putting the past behind us. I was strong and clear enough to maintain my own energetic presence and feel stable in being my true self. I had grown my roots deep enough and was able to reconnect and rebuild those relationships successfully enough to allow my children to know and appreciate their grandparents, as they were no harm to them.

For most of us, uprooting ourselves can be our choice, yet occasionally we are uprooted against our will. My adopted son's story is a poignant example of this. At age 15, he came to stay with our family for a few nights while his mother left town for a few days. His three-night sleepover turned into never going back to his mother's home. When she returned, she lost custody, due to drug problems and neglect. This severe experience tore and scarred this teenage boy's energy center to such a degree that for the next 15 years, he could not easily get on his own life path and purpose.

If you have a similar story of not having a choice or not being informed of a dramatic life change at any time in your life, this experience can leave an energetic scar in your root chakra energy. In the exercises at the end of this chapter, you will learn how to plug the energetic cord of your root chakra into your foot chakra. This can be difficult if you do not even have an energetic cord. So before you do the plugging-in exercise, envision a cord of energy, like a root growing out of the bottom of your torso, a thick and strong root that keeps growing until it can plug into your foot chakra and the earth. Underneath the energetic plate you are standing on, see deep roots growing into the ground. These are your roots, not anyone else's—not your family's or society's. By becoming deeply rooted in who you are as an individual, you can actually interact better in group and community experiences.

HOW DEEPLY ROOTED ARE YOU TO YOUR OWN TRUTH?

If your parents encouraged you to try new things, develop talents and skills, explore your world, travel, move out on your own, pursue a career and to use money as a tool during your developmental years, you were supported in establishing strong roots with your self-identity and purpose. Continue developing them.

If you moved frequently as a child, you would have experienced only growing shallow energetic roots. As an adult, that looks like having to make a greater effort in applying yourself in anything you do as you do not have a strong connection with a deeper energy of your purpose. You were not given the opportunities to grow deep roots as a child, but you have the opportunity to grow them now.

If you experienced physical, emotional, or sexual abuse, you would have not developed a deep root system. Abuse keeps you from feeling safe in the world, and when you don't feel safe in the world, you do not want to be here. When you don't want to be here, you cannot grow deep roots. Abuse creates a scarring energetic interference that keeps someone from feeling safe even into their adult life when there is no more risk of abuse. To grow your roots, use the plug-in exercise taught at the end of this chapter and see deep roots growing underneath your feet, into the earth. Now that you know more about the root chakra, you are ready to clear the old energy and activate the new energy into your life.

Exercises to Strengthen the New Energy of the Root Chakra

Use any and all of the following exercises to help you ground the new energy of the root chakra into your personal energy system. You can use them as frequently as you find supportive.

Plugging the Root Chakra Into the Foot Chakra

Close your eyes and take three deep breaths. Focus your attention on the bottom of your torso, the area between your legs. See a cord of energy coming down from your pelvic floor, just like an electrical cord that has a plug at the end of it. Look down at the plate of energy that is lighting up around your feet. See a plug that you can plug the cord into. Literally bend over and pretend you are plugging the cord into the outlet, connecting your root chakra with your foot chakra. See deep roots growing down into the earth below your feet, grounding and rooting you to your true self and your life path. Look up and see a path lit up in front of you with signs and markers designed specifically for you to show you the way along your path.

Energy Sketch Your Ideal Life Path

Energy sketching is a powerful and creative way to shift energy and visualize a different experience. Using markers and a piece of sketch paper, draw a stick figure of yourself on one side of the page. Draw a life path as you are now experiencing it extending out from you, regardless of whether or not current circumstances are what you want to experience. Sketch the feeling of the obstacles and challenges you are currently experiencing. Which patterns do you keep recreating on your path? Draw some of those patterns out. Use any of the following references to help you get started:

- **Losing your footing:** Draw the stick figure looking like you are stumbling.
- **Feeling lost:** Draw your path out in the distance, as if you cannot find it.

- **Obstacles in your way:** Draw rocks on your path that your feet are stuck in.
- **Feeling exhausted:** Draw your path as a mountain that is exhausting to climb.
- **Barely keeping your head above water:** Draw yourself having fallen off a cliff, far from your path, sinking in water.

To shift the energy in your root chakra, now create a second drawing of the new experience you are choosing to create with your root chakra energy. Draw a circle around your feet, representing your foot chakra. Next, draw a path extending out to you into the future. Draw roots growing deep into the earth creating a sense of being grounded and rooted to your truth. Draw the opposite of what you drew in your first drawing to help the energy start to shift, which patterns do you want to create on your path? Draw new, healthy patterns or write "I am" statements to declare the new patterns you are creating. For example:

- **Instead of losing your footing:** Draw roots under your feet so you create the experience of being stable and constant.
- **Instead of feeling lost:** Draw your path extending right out in front of you with you on it.
- **Instead of obstacles in your way:** Draw a large, wide-open path, free of rocks and debris that you can walk forward on effortlessly.
- **Instead of feeling exhausted:** Draw your path to be on even ground where you can easily walk forward.
- **Instead of barely keeping your head above water:** Draw yourself on solid ground with support to help you along the way.

You can write affirmations, or draw road signs and markers with supportive phrases. You can draw other people, or angels and guides helping you on your path. You can draw the currency symbol representing money showing up for you on your path. Draw hearts and other animated shapes that represent your heart's desires. After you have completed your sketch, imagine this energy being activated in your root chakra.

Easy Visualization to Stop Repeating Dysfunctional Patterns

Every day, you have approximately 16 hours that you are awake and on your life path. What are you allowing onto your path each day? How does your journey on today's path look the same as the days gone by? What challenges are you still dealing with that you were dealing with yesterday, a month ago? A year ago? Five years ago? Is your path like a treadmill or a hamster wheel, where you are caught in the illusion of moving with no forward progression?

Close your eyes and see yourself on a treadmill or a hamster wheel. Notice how fast you are moving and how it can be hard to keep up with the pace. You look down and realize you are not moving forward but are stuck in the same place, regardless of how much energy you expel. It felt like you were going forward! You certainly expended a lot of energy! Imagine a stop button that you can push. Push it! The treadmill or hamster wheel slowly comes to a complete stop. You take a deep breath and choose to get off of it. You are now free to move forward and make the changes that are timely and supportive for you. Declare the affirmation: *My efforts make a difference in changing the patterns in my life that no longer serve me to healthy functional patterns.*

Grounding Your Roots With Essential Oils

Massage a few drops of essential oils into the area of the 1st chakra on the hip bones. Carol Tuttle Healing Oils are custom blends that support you with specific healing goals. These oil blends can be used to activate and strengthen the root chakra in the following ways:

- **I am connected:** This oil assists you in staying in your own energy as you interact with others throughout your day. It strengthens your connection to your own energy field and the earth's energy field, so you can stay grounded and connected.
- **I am grounded:** This oil will support you in staying grounded and present in your body. As a result, your body will be empowered to activate its natural healing responses and functions to help the body heal and stay healthy.

What key thing did you learn from this section?

Use this space to make notes. Write down questions and insights you had while reading this section.

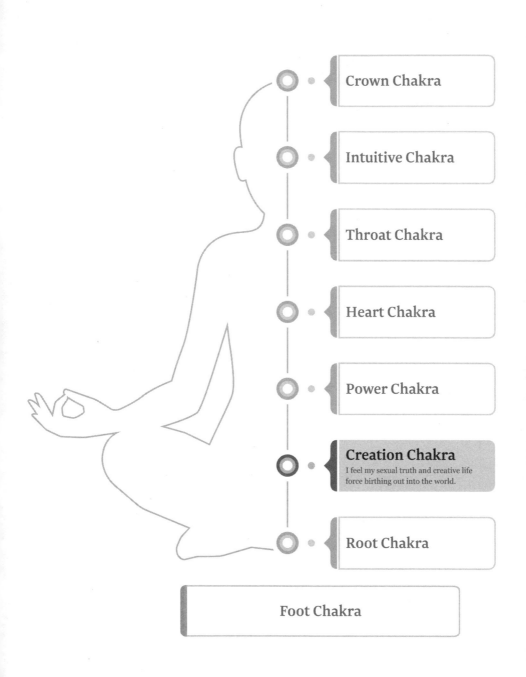

Crown Chakra

Intuitive Chakra

Throat Chakra

Heart Chakra

Power Chakra

Creation Chakra
I feel my sexual truth and creative life force birthing out into the world.

Root Chakra

Foot Chakra

Step 2: Expressing Your Sexuality and Creativity

· · · · · · ·

2nd Chakra—The Creation Chakra

Location:	In the middle of the belly or mid-back.
Yin/Yang Flow:	Yang, which feeds us with a drive to procreate and create in our lives.
Universal Color:	Orange
Associated Organs and Body Parts:	Reproductive organs, bladder, lower abdomen. Imbalance in this chakra can manifest physically as urinary infections, hip problems, and issues with reproductive processes.
Function:	Energetically feeding our drive to create and experience pleasure and passion.
Old Energy:	Sex is shameful and I have to give up pleasure to be spiritual.
New Energy	It is spiritual to feel pleasure and delight in the flow of life! Celebrating our sexual and creation energy.
If Closed:	You have shame energy in reference to sex and your sexuality. Sexual intimacy stirs up shame for you. You feel taken advantage of and unsupported by others. You put off creative endeavors and feel guilty if you have too much pleasure.
If Open:	You enjoy pleasure in many different ways in life. You create healthy sexual experiences that honor you. You have a powerful creative energy that is fed by your passion to make a difference in the world.
Affirmation:	I feel my sexual truth and creative life force birthing out in to the world.
Carol Tuttle Healing Oil Blends:	I am nurtured I am present

The second step in awakening brings us into the creation chakra energy, more popularly known as the sacral chakra. I have chosen to call it the creation chakra, as that reference more fully describes the function of the new energy of this energy center in our modern experience. Sacral refers to the sacrum, which is the area of the body this chakra vibrates from. This chakra has also been frequently referenced as the chakra that influences our sexual experience. Sexuality is definitely part of its function, yet not limited to that. Only seeing this chakra as related to sexual energy is a limiting view of the full power and influence of this energy center. I invite you to think in broader terms of creating that which brings you pleasure and birthing it into the world.

For example, let's start with the one experience of having sex. This can be an act purely for immediate pleasure, for strengthening an emotional and energetic bond between partners, or an act for creating a child, or all of these. All are creations that are designed ultimately to bring you pleasure. Think of the other millions of opportunities available to you that enroll you in the act of creating, birthing, and pleasuring in an experience. Here are simple examples: planning a vacation, going on the vacation, and enjoying yourself while on the vacation is an act of creation that brings pleasure. Choosing your next book, taking time to read the book, enjoying yourself while reading the book, is an act of creation and pleasure. The list of potential pleasurable, creative activities goes on and on: making a meal, building a career, cultivating important relationships. The question is: are you choosing to create and find pleasure in your creations that matter to you, free of guilt and shame?

The lower three chakra energies influence our physical experience in the world—our outer experience. Humanity has been primarily held in the energetic construct of the hierarchy of power and control. In other words, in our societies, the few have had great power and they controlled the masses' rights and choices. Until our modern times, humanity was limited in which pleasurable experiences could be chosen openly or even afforded. We have more rights and choices than ever before, yet many people still suffer from the old energy that keeps them from creating a life of affluence, joy, and pleasure. Let's change that so you no longer have to believe that to be spiritual, you have to go without!

THE OLD ENERGY OF THE CREATION CHAKRA

The old energy of the 2nd chakra heavily focused on sex. Unfortunately, sex has been shamed, guilted, messed up, misused, and misunderstood for centuries. In the past, most of the world's societies were heavily influenced by strict religious guidelines, and pleasure was categorized as sinful. We are now waking up to the truth that sex is a personal choice that we can take ownership of and that we want a pleasurable, healthy experience with. Unfortunately, since the primary source of the stigma and shame associated with sex historically came from religion, religion is now sometimes given a bad rap. But it is not religion's fault. The new energy of this chakra is helping us sort out the shame.

I recently asked some of my online Healing Center students to share their experience with religious shaming and sexuality. Here are just a few of many experiences that they shared. Which ones do you relate to?

"I came from a tradition that shamed female sexuality and especially shamed menstruation as well. It was reading Eastern and tantric texts, taking partner yoga classes and tantric yoga courses that enabled me to let go of some of the physical shame."

"I feel very closed energetically, especially in the second and fifth chakras. I shared things about my abuse with my husband

last night that I have never shared verbally (because it came up emotionally for me after posting). I woke up feeling very raw and my throat was closed up."

"My libido levels hover around zero. Yes, there is a history of sexual abuse, but I think it has more to do with religious shaming, especially as it relates to arousal. In the religious construct I was raised in, a great deal of effort and emphasis is placed on suppressing arousal and desire before marriage. I think I adopted the subconscious belief that arousal is bad because when I experience it in settings other than during intimacy, it triggers emotions of shame. I go in waves where I will take an interest in sexuality in the effort to try new things and figure this thing out but I quickly tire of the effort. My intention is to heal this issue."

Along with the religious shaming of sex and sexuality, the experience of sexual shame has also been created from the sexual abuse, rape, childhood molestation, sexual harassment, and women being pitched as sexual objects in media. The old belief that a woman's job is to pleasure a man comes from the era of a woman having no right to say no to sex to her husband in numerous cultures and times in history. All of these experiences are old energetic imprints that were created by a lesser-evolved humanity, influenced by the old energy of the 2nd chakra. The good news is, as the chakra energy evolves, we evolve with it and we choose creations of a higher consciousness. The chakra energy didn't create this; it was the lack of consciousness on the part of mankind that took this energy and created a version of power and control, shame, and abuse with this energy.

Of all of my chakras, I experienced the most wounding and improper development of my 2nd chakra. My sexuality energy was shut down for the first 30 years of my marriage. I participated in sexual intercourse and sexual intimacy but never experienced orgasm. Decades into my marriage, I rarely wanted or desired sex. In fact, because of all the shame and anger that was attached to sexual pleasure while I was doing it, I resisted and resented having sex.

I wanted to change this energy because it caused a lot of conflict in my marriage and within myself. I took the time for therapy and healing work to allow this energy to open. In my case, healing came through self-arousal and self-pleasuring as a critical part of the healing process. It took me until I was 54 years old to have my first orgasm. Why? Because when you don't want to feel the deep shame and anger that is intertwined with sexual arousal, you avoid sex and orgasm. Choosing to create my own arousal on my own, to clear the shame and anger, and to have my first orgasm by myself with myself was one of the most spiritual moments of my life!

Along with clearing the shame and anger that I carried both emotionally and in my body, I had to then address the deep sadness and grieve the many years of sexual pleasure I lost, due to the events of my childhood that damaged and scarred my 2nd chakra and my body's natural impulses.

I have now healed all that. I no longer have sex thinking it is just for my husband and I no longer do it if I think that it is necessary for him. It's always for me first.

My husband has been incredibly supportive of me doing this through literally three decades of healing work. I hope to shorten that timeline for you by quite a bit! My husband didn't enter our sexual experience together free and clear of shame residue either, as he had his fair share of sexual wounding through religious shaming. You can read both our stories in detail in my book, *Mastering Affluence* in the section on "How to Create Relationship Affluence."[23]

Most women and men have sexual wounds to heal as a result of the shame associated with sex through many generations. Even if you have not personally experienced sexual wounding via religious shaming or abuse, there is a good chance someone in your family ancestral line did and you inherited the energetic imprints that still need to be healed. (If you want more in-depth help beyond the exercises to strength the 2nd chakra at the end of this chapter, clearing sessions at The Carol Tuttle Healing Center can help you clear additional sexual wounding easily.)

"Sex is bad" is not the only old-energy paradigm that we are healing from the 2nd chakra. We also hold an old collective belief that too much pleasure, enjoyment, or fun represents laziness, pride, sinfulness, and worldliness. In centuries past, people took on the belief that you were more noble or worthy if you suffered more. That old energy is also being called up, accounted for, and healed.

The one event that leaves energetic imprints in your 1st and 2nd second chakra energy that could throw your life into patterns of unnecessary struggle is your birth. Your birth was your first physical event. It left an imprint on you. Depending on how that experience went, it left an old energetic stain in your root and creation chakra—the two energy centers of your mother that you moved through in the event of your birth.

Is birthing new experiences ever a struggle for you? The old energy of struggle imprinted in your 2nd chakra as a by-product of your birth is one of the primary reasons. Imagine what it is like to give birth, or think back to when you may have given birth. I think you will recognize the similarity of the old energy of struggle that is associated with our births and the struggle energy we can recreate in our birthing process of manifestation. Do you sabotage yourself, run into blocks and issues that make it more difficult, push through them believing it is just part of the process? Do you ever feel stuck, trapped, unable to move forward, pushing, overwhelmed, without support? Are your creations not valued or wanted? Those are all birth energy effects.

A few examples shared by my online clients shows you how your birth experience can set you up for specific patterns of struggle through-out your life:

> *"The only thing I've been told about my birth is that the hospital caught on fire and my mother was left standing out in the cold with a brand new baby (in South Dakota in the middle of December). A woman was smoking in bed and fell asleep. The indirect message I was receiving was, you will have struggle and it will be the direct result of someone else's bad choices. You won't have any control of the struggles that come to you."*

> *"Every time my birth is referenced it is about how huge I was, weighing 12.5 lbs at birth. One of my biggest challenges that I've dealt with in my life is feeling like I am a big burden to people. I realized that I felt this way about my birth story. I wouldn't come when my mother wanted me to. Because of that, I got too big. A common response when people discover my birth weight is, 'your poor mother.'"*

> *"My issue wasn't about the actual birth. It was about the time period before birth. My dad was military and my parents were overseas. My mom tested positive for TB. She didn't have TB, but her mother apparently died from it and my mom always tested*

positive for it. The doctors in France didn't know what to do about it so she was sent back to the states where she had to be in a TB isolation ward… So because of me she was separated from her family, and my brother was separated from his mother. This was never really a conscious thought, but when I did the clearing I was so emotional and tearful. Maybe this has had some hidden effect on me all these years."

In today's world, we have shifted the experience of birth in many ways that have removed the struggle energy from this original life experience. Mothers and fathers have more say as to where they want their children to be born. It's often a partner experience, commonly with both parents present. Fewer drugs are used, midwifery and doula care are becoming more common choices that create a more natural experience for the birthing mom. Water births, at-home births, more comfortable and homey birthing rooms in hospitals, along with babies staying with their moms, are all manifestations of 2nd chakra energy helping us create birth as a joyous experience that is supported with more awareness and ease.

You have the power to clear the old energy of your birth and no longer carry any energetic effects that have caused unnecessary suffering. As you clear the old birth energy from your 2nd chakra, you free yourself to learn how to create and birth pleasurable experiences. As you become the original creator of your story that was birthed into this world, you will be free to write your own story of what brings you pleasure and joy.

THE NEW ENERGY OF THE CREATION CHAKRA

The energetic shift that is taking place in the creation chakra is birthing an independence of our passion, sexuality, and creation energies—who we are sexually, what we want to experience with that energy, and how we create and birth that which brings pleasure into our lives.

The following are indicators that the new energy of the 2nd chakra is getting activated for you. How many of these have you experienced?

- You are tired of shaming your appearance and your body and want to think positive thoughts about yourself.
- You struggle with a low libido and know that there are other options to increase your sexual drive, but are not sure how to help yourself with changing this.
- You have a different sex drive than your partner and are frustrated with this. You want to find a way to work it out together.
- You feel sexually dysfunctional and think you are alone dealing with these struggles.
- You feel like you need to please your partner and are tired of feeling this way.
- You have ideas and passions you want to pursue, but you continuously do not give yourself the time to move forward and you easily come up with excuses as to why you can't.
- Deep down, you are afraid of failing at what your creative juices are encouraging you to do. You don't want to waste time and money if it isn't successful.
- You still feel guilty if you have too much pleasure and fun in your life, with a nagging feeling that you better get back to work and get something done. You want to experience pleasure as a positive in your life.

- You struggle with fertility issues, urinary tract infections, and digestive problems and are actively seeking answers to resolve these issues.

If any of those experiences feel familiar, you are ready for a shift. The 2nd chakra is expanding in its role in what it can support us in experiencing in life. This energy center has been the primary energy to fuel our sexual experiences. Unfortunately, because humanity has played in the energies of power, control, and struggle for centuries, this energy was used to create sexual shame, dominance, and control—mostly over women and people who are not heterosexual in their orientation. As humanity is waking up to higher states of consciousness, the 2nd chakra is also evolving in its role in what it can help us create and experience. The 2nd chakra is shifting from primarily influencing our sexual experience to supporting us in the experience of creating that which brings us pleasure overall. It does start with your sexual energy and what that sets into motion.

HOW IMPORTANT IS YOUR SEXUAL ENERGY?

If you were sexually abused, assaulted, bullied, if you were shamed by religious influences that told you sex is bad, if you have been alive on the planet for more than 10 years and been influenced by modern media, or if you come from a line of people who experienced *any* of this, you have sexual wounds! Yup, pretty much everyone! Including men! Men who were not held or touched enough in their infancy and toddler years come into their adult life subconsciously believing that sex is love, that sexual intimacy is the number one indicator that they are wanted. It's all just an effort to fill an unmet need to know that they are loved and wanted by the primary woman in their life. When Mom did not give this to her son, the adult female partner gets enrolled by the man's wounded inner child to make up the difference. It never works and it only sets a woman up to feel the old energy of, "all I am wanted for is sex."

The new energy of the 2nd chakra is about sexual ownership and freeing this energy up from all the other emotional jobs it has been given for men and women. Women get to heal the abuse, shame, and used energy. Men get to heal the need, dominance, and control energy that their sexual energy has been playing out.

The thought came through me that if we interviewed sexual energy about what it wants to support us with, the conversation would go something like this:

Interviewer: Hello, Sex. You've been playing a lot of roles in humanity with your energy being used for so many functions that seem unhealthy. How do you feel about that?

Sexual Energy: You're right, it's nice that humans are evolving so my energy can be used for more creative pleasures, not just sexual intimacy, but also for all creations that have the potential to be birthed into the world.

Interviewer: What do you mean by all creations being birthed as a result of your energy influencing them?

Sexual Energy: My energy is a creation energy. All things start as an idea and then the idea needs to be born into the world to become an object or an experience. I work very closely with the 6th chakra, where the ideas first come from. Ideas are then sent to me down the chain of the chakra energy to put my energy behind. This creates a drive in the person to take action and start to materialize the idea in physical form in the world.

Interviewer: That is so fascinating. I didn't realize that the chakras worked in partnership with each other. Can you tell me more about that?

Sexual Energy: Sure. The root, creation, and power chakras, (1st through 3rd chakras) are the energy centers that influence the physical world. The heart chakra (the 4th chakra), is the bridge to the upper chakras, throat, intuition, and crown chakras, (5th through 7th). The root chakra partners closely with the throat chakra, standing and speaking your truth. The creation chakra works closely with the intuitive chakra, birthing the ideas that come from inspiration. And the power chakra works closely with the crown chakra, using your personal power for good as you receive power from on high. The heart chakra is the bridge that connects the outer energy, lower chakras, with the inner energy, upper chakras.

Interviewer: How do you know so much about the entire chakra system?

Sexual Energy: I am the creation chakra. It's my job to make sure all the energy is flowing and moving. I am like a command center for the entire system.

Interviewer: You have a very important job. What happens when you are weak, dysfunctional, or blocked?

Sexual Energy: If my energy is weak and blocked, nothing works to your potential in your life. You compromise, but tell yourself it's not that bad, things could be worse. If my energy is dysfunctional and on overdrive, you become fixated on sex and needing more sex to feel alive, which is too narrow a focus for what my energy is meant to influence.

Interviewer: What does it look like if your energy is healthy and balanced doing the job it's designed to do?

Sexual Energy: When my energy is in balance, you have a positive and healthy experience with your sexual experience. You take care of your body and know your body's sexual prompts and you create positive, healthy experiences with sex that bring you pleasure. You have open and honest communication about your sexual experience with your partner and see the proper role it plays in your relationship as a fun and pleasurable activity, like so many other pleasurable activities you create together. You are in tune with and receive inspiration from your intuitive chakra about ideas, opportunities, and experiences you want to create and birth into your life. You feel a drive to take action on these ideas and have a passion for the process of creation, birthing, and seeing things materialize as a result of your efforts. You learn and grow in this process and continue to expand and explore who you are in the creation process. You know there is no bad experience or failure in what you pursue, as you know it is all a process of learning.

Interviewer: Thank you for your insights and the knowledge you have shared.

Sexual Energy: You are welcome, it's my "PLEASURE" to help you (pun intended)!

My biggest a-ha here is that sexual energy wants to be used for more than just sex! It is a creation energy, starting with its most primal role of creating more humans! What is your sexual energy wanting to create?

THE ROLE OF SEXUAL ENERGY IN THE CREATION PROCESS

(DISCLAIMER: I am a heterosexual woman who is in a monogamous relationship with my husband of 39+ years. What I share here is meant to help you understand the expanding role of the 2nd chakra energy. I am not supporting or promoting any particular sexual orientation or choice when it comes to individual or partner sex. I leave that to the reader's discretion to apply their own sexual orientation and value system to what I am teaching about the chakra energy.)

The experience of orgasm has been singled out to be the ultimate experience in the sex act. But what if it affected so much more in your life than just that? As I have vulnerably shared, I did not experience sexual orgasm until I was in my 50s. For decades, I told myself it wasn't that big of a deal, as it was just a small portion of my day-to-day experience that I was missing out on in my sexual experiences with my husband. When I started to become more aware of the many other benefits that orgasm contributed to my life in terms of health and manifestation, I was highly motivated to turn on this energy in my system. In fact, I can honestly say that I was much more motivated by those other benefits than by mere pleasure.[24] Which of the following would you like more of?

- Improved quality of sleep
- Glowing skin and anti-aging benefits
- Curbed appetite
- Prostate cancer prevention
- Immune system boost
- Stress relief
- Improved mental health

Beyond physical health, in the area of helping you manifest your desires, the energy of orgasm fuels what you are creating in life. Just as sexual intercourse is the original event that creates a human life, the energy of the 2nd chakra can be used to help us create other things in our lives. This does not mean you need to have sex to tap into that energy, but having a healthy sexual experience does help tremendously. Having a healthy sexual experience and being an active creator of your life work together—both experiences support the other.

My husband, Jon, is a man who had to heal the misperception he had that sex was an indicator that he was wanted and loved. He did not receive enough touch and caressing in his infancy and childhood, as his mother was often absent and had five other children to care for. He subconsciously tried to meet that unmet emotional need through sexual intercourse, which is a dysfunctional use of sexual energy. He also was challenged in pursuing his own dreams in taking steps to create his desires in his life. He was always supporting someone else or telling himself he couldn't do what he wanted—and he certainly couldn't just do it for the pleasure of it! As Jon healed his emotional needs and started to practice having sex with me from a place of sharing a pleasurable experience together, he also made a shift with pursuing more of the personal desires he wanted to create in his life. When he felt the urge that he "needed" sex to meet an unmet emotional need, he would direct that energy into something he was passionate about to help create more of it. As a result, his 2nd chakra energy is being used in a way that is beneficial to both his sexual and creative experiences.

Since I have balanced my sexual energy and opened the fullness of it, I marvel at the list of what I have been able to create. In just eight years I have written three books, launched new online learning and healing platforms, de-aged myself at least ten years in my appearance, and much more. For many of my long-term online followers, it has been obvious that I look healthier and younger than I did ten years ago. Some have thought I had a facelift! No. And I'll say this here, as I am not quite so forthcoming online to keep dispelling those rumors with the truth: I started orgasming!

WHEN PASSION ISN'T PLEASURABLE

It's one thing to know that pleasure is worthwhile and important, but it's another to actually experience it. What do you do if you're not experiencing pleasure in your passions? I am referring to two aspects of experiencing passion: the first is sexual passion that is not pleasurable on a physical and emotional level, and the second are passions in your life that present you with challenges as you pursue them.

The first challenge of not experiencing sexual passion as pleasurable presents you with an opportunity to find out what is causing the displeasure. For women, is it a dry vaginal area? Do you have a low libido due to hormone imbalances? Do old abuse energies get triggered that interfere with your present day experience? For men, are you dealing with sexual wounding, performance insecurities, or physical imbalances that could be addressed? Do you think sex is a way to satisfy your emotional wounding of not feeling good enough? Rather than just settle for unpleasant sexual experiences, make a decision that you are going to find what is causing the displeasure and change it.

If you are like me and did not experience the proper development of your sexual energies and bodily functions, you may feel challenged about wanting to have sex. You just don't get the urge because you carried the energy of shame or abuse that shut you down for so many years of your life. I'll share how I've worked through that so you can create the desire to have sex. First, my husband and I schedule sex. We both are mature enough to understand that in the busy lives of two adults who have been married for 39 years, you don't wait for impulses, especially if one of the two of us tends to not have them frequently out of nowhere. When we first started scheduling sex, it would be common for me to start to fret or resist that upcoming plan. My body had a habit of needing to protect itself. I've since switched that experience to support me in wanting to have sex. Here's how: a day or two before, I will set the intention that I will want to have sex and throw the energy forward to that time on my timeline so the energy can start to grow and support me in that outcome. To do that yourself, picture a timeline and throw the energy of desire onto it at the correct time. It's so simple, but it works every time and it makes both of our lives easier. In the exercises at the end of this chapter, I include a step-by-step technique to send your inner child away. I recommend this exercise if you have resistance to sex that you want to clear.

The other challenge of passion not being pleasurable refers to the experience of pursuing your dreams and passions—what you feel called or motivated to do in your life, in the areas of personal growth, career, and life mission. Just because you are pursuing a passion does not mean it will be pleasurable 100% of the time. You will need to overcome obstacles, address fears, and move through resistance from yourself.

The displeasure may come from having to put in more hours than you want to in order to make it happen, or needing to make sacrifices. I have personally experienced most of the above in the pursuit of my dreams and fulfilling my life mission. The challenges are temporary and as the saying goes: it's worth it. Continue to make the necessary adjustments in your thinking to support you in pursuing your passions and dealing with the challenging phases more honestly.

TAKING OWNERSHIP OF YOUR SEXUAL ENERGY

Another significant shift in the 2nd chakra that is helping us awaken is taking ownership of our bodies and sexual energy for both women and men. Again, the history of this shift goes back to the 1960s, as women's rights became a national movement. Two books written in the decades after that helped women learn about their bodies and their sexuality and also gave exposure to sexual abuse and assault: *Women's Bodies, Women's Wisdom,* by Dr. Christiane Northrup,[25] and *Courage to Heal,* by Ellen Bass.[26] As women have reclaimed their bodies and their sexuality, men have been helped and even forced to take accountability for the perceptions, actions and choices they have subjected women to, based on old energy paradigms that have influenced them.

Learn about your own body and what pleasures you. Self-healing and self-discovery are an important part of taking ownership and care of your body and your sexual energy. If you carry old shame energy around masturbation, I invite you to heal that shame and free yourself to claim back your sexual energy. For many people, just reading or speaking the word *masturbation* triggers deep reservoirs of shame. Does it make you feel dirty, unclean, or even evil? Learning about your body and its sexual function is a healthy pursuit. Sexual self-discovery and self-care in the form of self-induced sexual pleasure is part of that practice.

Some people connect the experience of masturbation with turning into an addiction. As with anything, sexual activities—whether with a partner sex or not—can become a negative, harming practice when out of balance. But anything taken to an obsessive extreme is unhealthy, even sweeping the floor. There is a lot of unhealthy and distasteful sexual content on the internet that can feed an addictive feeling of needing to masturbate. It's just readily available in our lives. But that distasteful content is not the full picture. A sexual addiction is just a sign of an unhealthy, imbalanced 2nd chakra. To find supportive resources to help you heal your sexual energy, set the intention that you will find the support you need in order to receive the pleasure that sexual energy is meant to enrich your life.

What is your next step in taking ownership of your sexuality? What is wanting to be created in your life that your 2nd chakra energy can support you with? Use the following exercises to activate your 2nd chakra, the creative chakra. Doing so will support you in having access to the energy your system needs to fuel your passion and creative drive to succeed in what you are moved to do in life.

Exercises to Activate the New Energy of the Creation Chakra

Use any and all of the following exercises to help you ground the new energy of the creation chakra into your personal energy system. You can use them as frequently as you find supportive.

Clearing Your Birth Energy

Birth is our original life experience. It sets up a pattern that creates pain and struggle in our lives. Clearing original birth energy releases us from this pattern and creates a new energetic pattern of affluence, ease, and joy.

1. Sit in a comfortable position with your arms and legs uncrossed.
2. Close your eyes and take three deep relaxing breaths.
3. Put your attention on your abdomen and your pelvic area; this is the space of your creation and root chakras.
4. Place your hand 8-12 inches off of your body in the area mentioned above and start rotating your hand in counter-clockwise rotations. As you rotate your hand, you will be unwinding and releasing your birth energy from your chakra energy.
5. Repeat the following statements to help you unwind and release your birth energy:
    *   Releasing, I am a bother, I am an interruption, others' needs are more important than mine, looking outside myself for validation, checking to see if the love is still there.
    *   Letting go of DNA patterns that keep me stuck in family dysfunction, feeling stuck, can't move forward, stuck in the birth canal, afraid to move forward, don't want to move forward, how can I survive?
    *   Releasing all of the times I have felt powerless, can't take care of myself, nobody is there for me, taking on my mom's energy, my dad is not there for me, not held or touched enough, problems at birth, not wanted, not the right sex, my needs are a stress to others. I can go without. Angry, frustrated, tired of living in this struggle energy.
    *   Let it all go once and for all. Take a deep breath and exhale and let it go.
6. Picture pulling all of the negative energy out of the chakra energy and sending it into the earth.
7. Imagine a color. Whatever color came to you, fill the area with that color.

8. Start rotating your hand in a clockwise direction to open and activate your chakra energy while repeating the following:

    *   I am wanted, I came at the right time, I deserve to have my needs met, my parents are grateful I am alive, I am a joy to others, I am loved and wanted, my needs are important, I am birthing new experiences that bring me joy, I easily receive that which brings me pleasure, I rejoice in my sexuality, I am a gift to this world.
    *   I am supported, I now choose to be born in the energy of love and joy, I am moving forward with ease, what I need and want shows up for me effortlessly, it's all there to support me, I stand in my truth, I pleasure in my life, I am creating my life and I pleasure in my results.
    *   I am creating success, I am creating wealth, I am creating a healthy body, I am creating joy-filled relationships. I pleasure in my success, I pleasure in my wealth, I pleasure my healthy body, I pleasure in my joy-filled relationships, I pleasure sharing my affluence with others. It is my birthright to thrive.

Making Figure 8s

Create a flow of energy between you and your partner by making figure 8's with your hand—moving your hand away from your body and then back toward your body in the shape of a sideways Figure 8. Do this energetic exercise physically or in your mind between your 2nd chakra and your partner's 2nd chakra.

Sending Your Inner Child Away!

If you are healing sexual shame and wounding from your childhood, use this technique to keep yourself from getting triggered or disassociated from your body when you have sexual intimacy.

Close your eyes and imagine yourself standing in the light. Bring into your visualization any higher power you are connected to, i.e. Christ, God the Father, God the Mother, Angels, Higher Self, Goddesses, etc. Consider this presence or presences as your spiritual support team in this visualization.

Invite your inner child of any and all ages that experienced sexual wounding. Share with them you are an adult now and want to have healthy intimate experience with your partner and they are not meant to be a part of it. Ask you spiritual support team to take this child to a safe place, away from the sexual event you choose to take part in as an adult.

Bring your attention back to your body, take three deep breaths, breathing deeply in to your whole body. Tell yourself, "I am an adult creating a healthy sexual experience for myself." Open your eyes and proceed with your sexually intimate experience.

Identifying What's Ready to Be Created

Without giving it much thought, answer the following question 10 times, with the first thing that comes to mind: "What are 10 things I want to create that I have been feeling a drive for?" You can write down your answers or say them out loud. It's okay to repeat yourself.

Having Creation Sex

Keeping sex interesting can be a challenge the longer you are married! Here's an idea to give it a whole new function. In the foot chakra section, I teach you how to do an energy circle to help energize your creation and attraction energy. What would that look like if you did the same thing with your sexual energy while you were having a sexual experience? Whether you are pleasuring yourself or having partner sex, set an intention of something you want to create more of by filling in the blank, "I am creating more..." Now let it go without thinking about *how* you will create that. You want to get out of your head and into your body. When you climax, that powerful energy will be channeled into your intention.

Working on Creative Projects

To activate and sustain your creative energies, make it a practice to be involved in something creative. You can do activities that are stereotypically seen as creative, such as painting or creating music. But also consider other activities that can be creative, too: making an intentional meal, planning an event or outing, or anything that is calling to be created. The options are endless. Choose something creative to do on a weekly basis.

Tapping Into Your Creative Powers With Essential Oils

Massage a few drops of essential oils on the location of the 2nd chakra on the abdomen, just below the navel. Carol Tuttle Healing Oils are custom blends that support you with specific healing goals. These oil blends can be used to activate and strengthen the creative chakra in the following ways:

- **I am nurtured:** This oil will help you heal negative energy imprints and wounding that you took on as a result of being abused or having to live in a toxic family environment
- **I am present:** This oil will assist you in staying present in your body when you are experiencing sexual intimacy. It is also useful to use when working on creative projects to activate the creative energies that contribute to the creation process.

What key thing did you learn from this section?

Use this space to make notes. Write down questions and insights you had while reading this section.

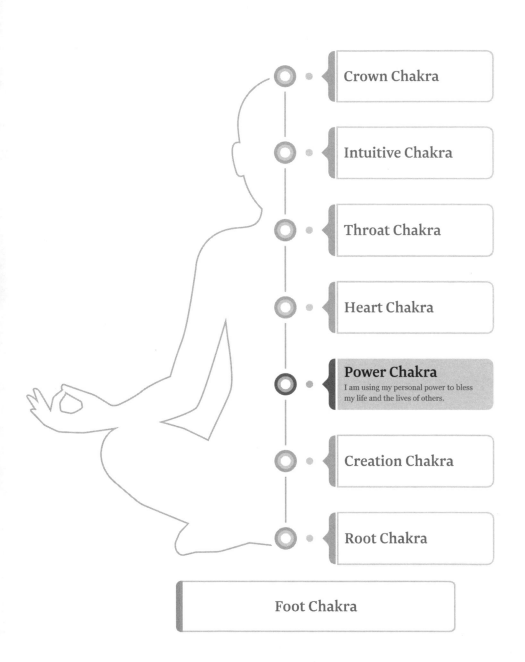

Crown Chakra

Intuitive Chakra

Throat Chakra

Heart Chakra

Power Chakra
I am using my personal power to bless my life and the lives of others.

Creation Chakra

Root Chakra

Foot Chakra

Step 3: Owning Your Personal Power

• • • • • • •

3rd Chakra—The Power Chakra

Location:	Below the sternum, above the belly button and mid-back.
Yin/Yang Flow:	Yang, with the energy moving outward to take action in the world.
Universal Color:	Yellow
Associated Organs and Body Parts:	Digestive system and lower back. Imbalances in this chakra can manifest physically as digestive issues or lower back pain.
Function:	Energetically connecting us to our authentic will, personal power, self-esteem and how we use it to create relationships and take action.
Old Energy:	I have to use my power to control or prevent from being controlled.
New Energy	I use my personal power to take inspired action and create equitable, collaborative relationships.
If Closed:	You give your power to others in an effort to keep the image of peace. You easily take on other people's energy. You feel blocked, unable to act or move.
If Open:	You have a strong sense of your own authentic power and how to use it in healthy ways. You use your power and influence for good in the world. You admire others with power and influence and choose to emulate people who use their personal power to make a difference in the world. You attract individuals who you can create healthy equitable, collaborative relationships with.
Affirmation:	I am using my personal power to bless my life and the lives of others.
Carol Tuttle Healing Oil Blends:	I am confident I am fit

The third step in awakening brings us into the power chakra energy. One of the most obvious shifts of energy is taking place in this energy center, due to a shift of the ages that is playing out.

Do you remember the song "Age of Aquarius/Let the Sun Shine In," released in 1969 by The 5th Dimension?[27] It was an instant hit and played in over 1,750 runs on Broadway in the popular musical, *Hair*. Most people know the chorus line of this song, even if they were not yet alive back then! Take a moment to google the song, pay attention to the lyrics, and sing along.

The message of this song was that we were leaving the "Age of Pisces" on the planet and entering the age of Aquarian energy—the "Age of Aquarius." What are these ages? They are defined by astronomical phenomena. The twelve astrological signs (Pisces, Aquarius, Scorpio, Capricorn etc.) are twelve constellations. For stretches of about 2000 years, the vernal equinox passes through a certain constellation. (The vernal equinox is the day during springtime when the sun crosses Earth's equator.) From approximately 0 A.D. to the present, this constellation has been Pisces.[28] As the angle of Earth's axis has shifted, as it periodically does, we are moving into Aquarius. Aquarius and Pisces overlap, which is one reason we have been in the transition from the Piscean Age to the Aquarian Age for the last 50 years .

Why is this so important? Because every person on planet Earth has been and will be affected by this shift. Let's investigate what will be changing as a result of the shift of energy occurring in the power chakra. The Piscean Age was characterized by hierarchy and power. For the past 2000 years, this dominant and subordinate arrangement of energy has been the foundation for human consciousness. Class systems, hierarchy, power and control were to be expected creations of this period. Everything that you have learned from your parents, and they from their parents, going back 2000 years, has been colored by this Piscean frame of reference. And now all that is changing.

In the world of metaphysics, it is taught that the Piscean Age is the time we experience the dominant and subordinate arrangement of energy. We really couldn't change our cultures or our personal family system constructs very easily until the Aquarian Age. The Aquarian age shifts the energy so that we instinctively use our personal power to create positive change, partnership, and goodwill.

When does the Age of Aquarius start? There is a lot of speculation and differing opinions on this, but I would say that we are definitely moving into it and the power chakra is helping us make changes from the old energy of power and control to the new energy of healthy personal power that makes a difference in the world and relationships.

THE OLD ENERGY OF THE POWER CHAKRA

Historically, many of the world's systems have been run from the power chakra's old energy construct of the few using power and control to dominate the many. These dominant and submissive roles were typical manifestations of the Piscean Age.

You can see how this pattern has played out in both healthy and unhealthy ways, on both the macro and micro levels of our lives. For example, on the macro level, governments, medical systems, political systems, religious systems, and other organizations have created an experience of the few having power and control over the majority, who must submit to it.

You can see unhealthy versions of this energy in governments oppressing their citizens, people losing faith in political and religious leaders due to acts of infidelity or lies, or modern medicine influencing many to turn to drugs to medicate, rather than teaching preventive approaches to our health. In all of those examples, people in authority maintain power under the guise of, "We will take care of you." This is the old energy of the power chakra that is now shifting to the point of power being inside of us. We are all learning to trust ourselves and our own power and authority.

Each of us will have life events present us with the opportunity to take back our power. If we do not choose it, then another scenario will present itself.

One of the first times I stepped into my personal power to take my and my family's power back happened when I was a young mother in my late 20s. My second child, my son Christopher was only 18 months old at the time and had experienced a series of ear infections. Up until this time, I believed that the doctor had all of the power and right to decide what was correct for my child, so I listened to him and did what he recommended without question.

With the increased frequency of ear infections and increased strength of each round of prescribed antibiotics, I felt more and more uncomfortable. I knew the medication was stripping away my son's own antibodies and weakening his immune system. By the time he'd had five ear infections within three months, I started to investigate on my own what could be the cause of his weakened immune system. This was in 1986, way before the internet, so research required me to visit the library. In a nutshell, I began to learn that food sensitivities could play a big role in weakening his immune system and provoking ear infections. At our next appointment for the next ear infection, I started to share with the doctor what I had been studying and learning. He quickly scoffed at me, dismissed my feedback, and shut down the conversation in a demeaning way. I was stunned! I picked up my son and told the doctor that I was not interested in giving my son another round of antibiotics, that we would not be coming back, and that I would find a doctor who would work with me. That day, I took my power back from modern medicine.

How did the story end? I did find a doctor who shared similar views, who worked with me, and listened to my feedback. He trusted that I was the authority of my own child and that a mother's intuition is powerful. He removed specific foods and put Chris on a protocol of supplements to rebuild his immune system. It took about nine months to get him healthy and stable. He stopped having ear infections, and to this day at age 34, he has no food sensitivities.

Don't get me wrong, I am not anti-modern medicine. Thanks to modern medicine, my youngest son is alive due to surgical intervention for pyloric stenosis at four weeks old, and my husband who had a stroke at age 55 was given the highest level of care so he did not have long term damage to his brain. The point is not medicine. The point is power. The lesson here is: Where is the point of power when it comes to large systems, organizations, and businesses for you? What are you still giving your power to? Review this list and circle the ones you still feel have more power than you:

- Medical system: Do you feel you have to have a doctor or medical professional give you permission to pursue alternative or complementary health approaches?
- Insurance industry: Do you believe you cannot seek health care if your insurance does not cover it?
- Government leaders and systems: Are you angry that you have to pay taxes? Do you shame and blame politicians?
- Religious systems: Have you left your religion in anger and upset? Do you think less of people who actively participate in their own religions?

- Economic system: Do you still believe that money has more power than you do? Do you feel powerless and scared at the mention of a recession?
- Educational system: Do you feel that people with higher degrees know more and have more expertise due to their degrees? Do you believe your children will not succeed without degrees from a college or university?
- Banks and financial systems: Do you feel as if financial systems are stacked against you or that you'll always be at the bottom?
- Beauty and fashion industry: Do you believe that you are unattractive? Do you shame your appearance on a regular basis?
- Health and diet industry: Do you eat the standard American diet? Do you get discouraged about never reaching your ideal weight?

Which of these macro experiences of your life are you still giving your power to? Can you think of others? The goal is to take your power back. That does not mean you are not willing to be compliant with or use these systems in your life. For example, if you do not pay your taxes as an act of taking your power back from government, you'll deal with some very unpleasant consequences. Taking your power back means that you are in charge of what's correct for you and you have the power to discern what that means in a given situation. In other words, you choose to pay your taxes from your own place of power, rather than feeling powerless and forced. In our societies, the point of power is shifting from being outside of us to the point of power being within us. As I will share in the next section of this chapter, we are taking our power back in big ways. Whatever is showing up in your life right now is inviting you to take your power back.

THE NEW ENERGY OF THE POWER CHAKRA

The energetic shift taking place in the power chakra is opening the space for us to all play on an even playing field in an equitable and honoring manner. We are learning to own our own power, to be accountable for our choices and actions, and to allow others to own their power and accountability. Collectively, we also feel more and more compelled to use our power to make a difference in the world.

As we learn to take accountability for ourselves and support others in being accountable for themselves, we create an opportunity to come into partnership with each other to collaborate and create equanimity and respect and create "the experience of the whole is greater than the sum of its parts."

The following are indicators that the new energy of the 3rd chakra is getting activated for you and you are feeling a deep sense of it being time to own your personal power. How many of these have you experienced?

- You are tired of giving away your power and apologizing for yourself. You are more aware than ever that you still do this as a habit at times.
- You struggle with low self-esteem, but logically you know there is no reason you need to anymore.
- You have done a lot of healing work, yet are still afraid to move forward. You want to move forward into action more easily.
- You are aware that you take on others people's negative energy and want some effective solutions to no longer do this.
- You are experiencing tension or conflict in your partner rela-tionship. You are feeling ready and willing to create a healthy

partnership with your significant other by being accountable for yourself and letting them be accountable for themselves.

- You are looking for clarity on how to use your power to make a difference in the world.

If you have experienced any of these, you are ready to connect with your authentic power and self-esteem. Think of a recent situation when you were aware that you gave your power away to someone else—an organization, a limiting belief, or even a bad habit. Now that you have that experience in mind, notice what it felt like. Did it feel like a drain of your energy? Where did you feel it in your body? What thoughts went through your head? How quickly did you notice that you gave your power away? You might have noticed before you did it, but then you did it anyway. Or you may have noticed while you were doing it, or afterward. Notice where you are at with this habit. Which situations are still challenging for you to stay true to your own power and authority?

This poem by Portia Nelson has been a favorite of mine for many years. When I first read it back in 1990, I realized it was teaching in metaphor the process of giving our power away, waking up, and changing that pattern. Understanding this progression of change helps us be more patient with the process.

Chapter I
I walk down the street
There is a deep hole in the sidewalk.
I fall in.
I am lost… I am helpless.
It isn't my fault.
It takes forever to find a way out.

Chapter II
I walk down the same street.
There is a deep hole in the sidewalk.
I pretend I don't see it.
I fall in again.
I can't believe I am in the same place.
But, it isn't my fault.
It still takes me a long time to get out.

Chapter III
I walk down the same street.
There is a deep hole in the sidewalk.
I see it is there.
I still fall in. It's a habit.
My eyes are open.
I know where I am.
It is my fault. I get out immediately

Chapter IV
I walk down the same street.
There is a deep hole in the sidewalk.
I walk around it.

Chapter V
I walk down another street.[29]

Consider the possibility that in this poem, the street you are walking down represents life experiences that are perfectly designed so you can learn how to stay true to your authentic power and identity. The deep hole represents your habit of giving your power away. You keep falling in that hole, first with the mindset that you are the victim with no other choice. Then you start waking up to the truth that you are creating this experience and are meant to learn from it. Then you learn you are connected to your true identity and power every day of your life. With that in mind, this is how it could read:

Chapter I
I walk down the street
There is a deep hole in the sidewalk.
I GIVE MY POWER AWAY
I am lost… I am hopeless.
It isn't my fault.
It takes forever to find a way out.

Chapter II
I walk down the same street.
There is a deep hole in the sidewalk.
I pretend I don't see it.
I GIVE MY POWER AWAY AGAIN
I can't believe I am in the same place.
But, it isn't my fault.
It still takes me a long time to get out.

Chapter III
I walk down the same street.
There is a deep hole in the sidewalk.
I see it is there.
I STILL GIVE MY POWER AWAY… IT'S A HABIT

My eyes are open.
I know where I am.
It is my fault. I get out immediately

Chapter IV
I walk down the same street.
There is a deep hole in the sidewalk.
I STAY IN MY OWN POWER

Chapter V
I walk down another street. I LIVE TRUE TO MY POWER AND
AUTHORITY EVERY DAY OF MY LIFE.

Which chapter are you currently living? Maybe you are in different chapters in different situations of your life. Wherever you are, you can guarantee the experiences will continue to manifest for you, walking down the street of claiming your power back, until you learn your new lesson of these truths: "As I live true to my authentic power, I can achieve both difficult and easy tasks with grace and ease. I am supported by life."

WHY WE GIVE OUR POWER AND AUTHORITY AWAY

Why can't we just live true to ourselves and stay true to our own power and authority? Logically, it seems reasonable to be able to do this while we honor what is right for others. Yet we often give our power away in an effort to satisfy unmet emotional needs and limiting beliefs.

In my work with millions of people both online and private practice through the years, I have identified the following five unmet needs and limiting beliefs as the biggest reasons we give our power away. If you have any of these beliefs either subconscious or consciously, you will be tempted to give your power away most times unknowingly until you take care of the unmet need and change the deeper belief.

- I have to please others to get my needs met.
- I will hurt feelings if I am not agreeable.
- I need to go along with the crowd so I don't draw attention to myself.
- I need to just go along to avoid an upset.
- What I want doesn't matter; my needs are not important.

These beliefs lead to habits that become life practices. Over time, we eventually don't even know that we are choosing or that we have an option to choose. We literally have no idea we have a problem. It's like stanza 1 of walking down the street. We fall in the hole we don't even know is there and we blame someone else for our compromised life experience.

Let's look at each of the five common limiting beliefs that give your power away, as well as what you can try instead:

"I HAVE TO PLEASE OTHERS TO GET MY NEEDS MET."

We learn this lie at an early age as children. Without vindictive motives, our parents actually require us to do this, as we are at their mercy to have our needs met, both emotionally and physically. When our needs are not met, we begin to alter our truth to comply with our parents' preferences, as they reward us for doing that. For that reason, this is a deeply held belief by most people. We continue to play out this pattern in our adult lives through the habit of thinking of what others want first and accommodating for what we assume they want so that they are pleased with us.

Every time we enact the habit of people pleasing, either consciously or subconsciously, we give our power away. We place ourselves in a subordinate position to the person we are pleasing and no longer interacting on an even playing field. If you only have your attention on what you think others want or expect from you, that is where your power goes—to them and the situation you are involved in. The more you become aware of this, you are sure to feel the energy leave your system.

Try this instead: Next time you begin to notice yourself thinking of others and trying to "please" them before you consider yourself, turn your attention inward and ask yourself, "Is this correct for me? Have I considered myself in this choice?" Sometimes the answer is no, and sometimes the answer is yes! Proceed or modify, based on your consideration of yourself. Your actions may not look too different on the outside, but the place you are coming from keeps your power intact rather than giving it away.

"I WILL HURT THEIR FEELINGS IF I AM NOT AGREEABLE."

Most of us have heard numerous times from various people that we hurt their feelings. Your mother may have said that to you in an effort to change your behavior. You may have had a boyfriend or girlfriend who responded to a breakup as though you had hurt them. My mother used her feelings as a disciplinary tactic to provoke her children to change. She wasn't blatant about telling us her feelings were hurt, but her mood made apparent that she was upset or saddened at times, due to our choices as children.

It is a common practice to receive or share feedback along the lines of "you hurt my feelings." The truth is, we have no power over anyone's feelings. Yet, due to this flawed belief, we give away our power in order to avoid or prevent the possibility that we might hurt someone's feelings.

When we give away our own power, we are actually hurt the most, as our energy is drained.

How many times have you chosen to do something that you really didn't want to do because if you didn't, you believed you would "hurt their feelings"? Even something as simple as cancelling a lunch date with a friend that just isn't working out?

Try this instead: When you are about to do something contrary to what is correct for you because you worry about making someone feel bad, remind yourself, "I am in charge of my feelings. They are in charge of theirs. Their feelings are not my business and when I do what is correct, it is best for everyone." Remember, you will feel more and more of an energy drain the longer you are aware that you have this habit and do not change it. Awareness creates accountability for choosing something different. It's like the Universe now knows you are aware and it ramps up the cause and effect of the situation to make it more and more uncomfortable for you to keep acting out your falling-in-the-hole strategies!

"I NEED TO GO ALONG WITH THE CROWD SO I DON'T DRAW ATTENTION TO MYSELF."

At times in your life when you chose to stay true to your authentic power, you may have experienced shame, embarrassment, harassment, or even violence from others. This backlash was painful and uncomfortable and may have caused you to resist ever doing it again. As the energy of the power chakra continues to open space for people to individually do what is correct for them, the more space there is for diversity and individuality. Trust that it is becoming safer and safer for you to do what is right for you.

Try this instead: The next time the fear presents itself and you worry that it's not safe to do what is right for you, tell yourself, "I am knowing when it is correct to do what is correct for me, and when I should be discreet for my own well-being." Using your discernment gives you permission to choose what is right for you, which honors your true power, rather than closing down out of fear to prevent what you don't want to happen.

"I NEED TO JUST GO ALONG WITH IT TO AVOID AN UPSET."

This belief starts to form in our grade school years, as we start to get into trouble from our parents at times for doing what we want! We were reprimanded, disciplined, told we couldn't do that. We may have taken on this belief in school because a teacher's feedback felt shaming, or peers called us out and embarrassed us, so we went silent. We may have upset our mom or dad, and we noticed that following our own true course was upsetting to others. We may have seen a sibling get in trouble and silently told ourselves we were not going to make choices that caused upsets. In order to avoid contention or upsets, we did or do what others want, rather than what is correct for us.

Try this instead: First, you need to change your belief that if you do what is correct for you, others will be upset. Change the belief to: "I am choosing what is correct for me and others support me." Make this shift in your thinking and it will shift your energy so that you can do what is correct for you. You will be amazed at the support that your new energy generates for you.

"WHAT I WANT DOESN'T MATTER; MY NEEDS ARE NOT IMPORTANT."

This belief can even begin in infancy! If we are not picked up or held enough this belief gets seeded and it is confirmed throughout our lives every time someone is dismissive of us. A by-product of this deeper belief is we stop considering what we want or need and no longer have a connection to our power chakra energy. There is no need for personal power as we do not have the esteem to use it.

Try this instead: Your daily mantra for a while needs to be, "What I want matters, my needs are important." It's a simple fix, but will take time for you to believe it. So say it over and over. Write it down and put it where you will see it often. This will start to generate a connection to your power chakra energy that will feed your self-confidence. When you esteem yourself as worthy and deserving, you have the self-confidence to use your power to go after what you want. Your life is important. You are important and that is not just my opinion. That is a fact.

When you claim your power back, powerful changes occur in your daily experience. Here's an example of what this can look like in your daily life, as described by one of my clients as she started to claim her power back:

"I have always been what is now referred to as a 'co-dependent' person. I have very willingly taken the blame for many things that were never my fault. 'Peace at any price' has been an unspoken law in my life. If anyone was unhappy, I found myself apologizing and trying to fix everything. When I was treated rudely, or if I felt my feelings were not considered, I would just smile and say, 'Don't worry about it. It's not that big of a deal.' I found it just about impossible to speak out when I felt uncomfortable.

As I have become stronger and my value as a person has become clearer, my personal relationships have changed dramatically. I will not allow myself to be disregarded anymore. My thoughts and feelings are just as important as those of others in the relationship. I have a right to say, 'Please don't use my things without asking,' or, 'I feel hurt when you say or do that to me.' To some this may seem very basic but it represents over a year of hard work to get to this place in my life.

I am learning to be more confident and assertive on the job. In the past, I was told by my co-workers that I didn't have much self-confidence and I know that some people doubted my ability to perform my daily tasks. As I grow stronger, I feel more confident and I know that I give that feeling to others, too. I feel less anxiety when I have to make decisions, or to perform tasks in a precise way. My confidence is growing every day. I am a much happier person. I know I am moving in the right direction one step at a time."

As this client's story shows, the power chakra energy is helping us to wake up and see that we have habits that no longer serve us. Whenever we fall back into these habits, this chakra shines its powerful energetic light on them. Being able to see and identify these unmet needs and limiting beliefs in ourselves gives us awareness. And when we have awareness, we can stop falling in the hole and eventually choose to walk down a different street.

IS SOMEONE STEALING YOUR POWER CHAKRA?

An interesting aspect of our chakra energy is that other people can tap into it and channel it from us. The most popular chakra that gets hacked by others is the power chakra. What I mean by "hacked" is that other people are actually using our energy to make up for the lack of energy in their own system. If someone else's power chakra is compromised,

141

they can unconsciously steal our energy to give them a sense of more power. This happens particularly if you are still running a dominant/ subordinate energy set-up in your intimate relationship or any signifi-cant relationship in your life, such as parent-child, employer-employee relationships.

Having personal boundaries creates an energetic protection and boundary around your chakra energy. Boundaries are limits that help give our lives structure and form. Boundaries offer us protection from the damaging words and actions of others and our own self-defeating behaviors. Boundaries help us to establish limits and guidelines that are necessary to maintain our personal energy and use this energy for ourselves rather than letting others steal it from us.

An example from one of my clients shows how setting boundaries and taking your power back can play out smoothly. As you read, pay attention to what insights you get about your own situation:

> *"My husband was in the habit of putting me down with sarcastic*
> *and negative comments. They were always loaded with humor*
> *and I had allowed myself to accept them through the years. He*
> *always claimed he was only kidding! Carol helped me understand*
> *that every time I did this I was allowing my husband to take*
> *my power away. What I didn't realize was due to his lack of*
> *confidence and his own compromised source of personal power as*
> *a result, this pattern of putting me down was a way he could get*
> *a false sense of power, using me as his power source! This was a*
> *game changer for me, I started to notice that when he did this, I*
> *would feel deflated and that he felt more energized!*

Carol coached me on how to set boundaries by using my voice and sharing with him what I wanted. At an arranged time that I had invited him to chat with me I told him that I wanted to share something that was very important to me. Rather than focusing on what I didn't want and what I believed he was doing wrong, Carol recommended I share what I wanted for me and for both of us, so I shared the following: 'I want a loving and supportive relationship with you and your teasing and making fun of me can be hurtful. I would appreciate it if you no longer did that.' He wasn't aware how hurtful his joking with me was. Why would he? I had never shared how it made me feel. Once he knew this he stopped the putdowns. This change helped us both connect with our own authentic power and use it to create a more cooperative relationship."

CREATING COLLABORATIVE INTIMATE RELATIONSHIPS

In order to create healthy and balanced relationships, where both people are honored and supported in being their authentic self, you have to be connected to your personal power source. If you are not connected to your personal power or do not allow your power to support you first, you are either giving your power away to others, or taking on other people's negative energy.

The 3rd chakra is like a powerhouse of energy that feeds us and sustains our sense of being our own person, in our own energy. As you activate your power chakra, you will change your relationship for the better. The new energy of the power chakra is designed to affect our relationships in a supportive way, giving us power to create collaboration and partnership. This is not just an abstract concept. It can affect real change in your relationship. Here is what it can look and feel like:

"I am noticing a calm in myself and willingness to be accountable for my share of the relationship problems. This week's power chakra exercises have been really powerful for me. I feel a new energy coming into our relationship—we are enjoying each other much more! I am noticing a calm in myself and willingness to be accountable for my share of the relationship problems. I am able to step away and look at myself first before talking to my husband and then I am able to speak clearly about what I need. I am amazed at the difference it has made in our relationship and how effortless it is shifting for both of us."

"I've noticed less blaming and more tenderness! We're starting to take responsibility for our own creations and beginning to choose wisely!"

Your power chakra energy supports you in taking responsibility in your relationship that you didn't know you had. When you believe you are accountable for all your thoughts, beliefs, and actions, you truly have great power to act. Those actions can't help but affect your relationship in positive ways.

FOLLOWING INSPIRED ACTION

Another huge benefit the power chakra feeds us is the energy of taking action and going after what is timely and correct in our lives. When the energy of our power chakra is strong and active, it is a point of attraction to draw into our lives what we are meant to respond to. This is a beautiful way to live, as you get into a rhythm of following energy and taking inspired action, rather than having to will yourself to move toward what you want. What is timely and correct finds you and you respond with action.

To strengthen your power chakra attraction energy, try this: Imagine what you want is looking for you. You don't even need to know what it is! You just know that when it shows up, it's going to be clear to you and you will respond by moving into action easily and effortlessly without hesitation.

Now, take your hand and put it in front of your power chakra, in the area of your sternum. Make a sideways figure 8 by extending your hand away from your power chakra, loop it down and back up, bringing your hand back to the starting point. Do this 7–8 times while you are thinking or speaking, "I am drawing to me what is timely and correct and when it shows up, I take action with confidence and ease."

USING YOUR POWER TO DO GOOD IN THE WORLD

Once you have a strong point of attraction and are in the momentum of bringing timely and correct opportunities into your life, you will start to notice that you are attracting more and more opportunities to do good in the world and make a difference. You power chakra wants to help you live your life purpose and one of those purposes is sharing your gifts to make a difference.

The new energy of the power chakra is stirring within us a poignant desire to share our gifts, to make a difference with humanity or the planet. Take a moment to consider what calls to you. Are you called to help other people? Are you being called to help the planet? What is your sense of where you are meant to use your gifts?

If you are not feeling a call, work on activating your power chakra, rather than trying to find your life purpose. Trust that within that practice is the energy to attract to you what you are trying to find right now.

Your purpose will find you and you will be amazed by how much better it is than anything you could imagine on your own!

SHIFTING FROM THE OLD TO NEW ENERGY OF RELATIONSHIPS

The stereotypical male/female relationship has played out for years out as a dominant/subordinate energy construct, with most relationships set up with the male playing the dominant role and the female playing the subordinate role. I recently received the following question from a member of The Carol Tuttle Healing Center:

"How do I heal being in relationships where men want to control me? I have found this to be a problem with many males in my life."

I shared the following insights that could be true for you, too:

"This is a very old energy that has most likely preceded you in previous generations. You are the one to change this old pattern completely. Due to old energies held in your 3rd chakra, you are still manifesting this in your relationships. You are not the author of these patterns, but you are still a carrier until you clear them and create new healthy patterns.

First, take a look at your childhood. Where is the evidence in your childhood that men were controlling? Was your father controlling to your mother? Was your father controlling in his parenting methods? What about your grandparents? How far back does this go? For your ancestors, it would have felt normal and correct to play in these roles, but since you are part of the current shift of the energies of the chakras, it does not feel supportive to you."

Another member asked this question:

"I would like help to clear the pattern of running my parents' relationship in my own relationship. I have a very supportive partner but I feel I'm playing out or responding to things like I saw my parents do in their relationship. I am very different from my mom but I seem to respond to things like I observed her do in her relationship with my dad: male is dominant, female is subordinate. It feels yucky."

In response to her question, I recommended that this client go through certain clearing sessions in the Healing Center. What she found was that claiming her personal power was actually very simple and possible in her everyday life. You can experience that, too, as you set the intention to take your power back. Here's the update this client shared:

"I became aware of how much of a people pleaser I am, how much I take on other people's energy. My pattern had become to hold how I really felt inside of me, telling myself it didn't really matter, when it really did matter to me, until I would then explode in anger. It dawned on me how easy it was to change and I just need to speak how I really felt and what I really wanted, to just say what I need, and to do it without exploding! I made myself start practicing this, and it felt so right to use my power and my voice to share what is correct for me. I look at how simple the solution has always been and am blown away at how much I

couldn't / wouldn't / shouldn't / didn't use my power in a healthy and appropriate way. I realize now it was getting harder and harder to keep it in, and the anger explosions were happening more frequently. I understand personally what Carol means when she says, "in the time in which we live it is harder to play out old patterns than to use our power to change them."

I recently chatted with my husband about my realizations and there were a lot of tears and accountability. I own it all as a fabulous creation of mine and am ready to release and embrace the new. Before Carol's healing support, I literally had no idea this was a problem, that not asking for help, expecting hubby to mind read my needs, being resentful when he or anyone else gets it wrong, then ending with a tantrum of 'See? I knew I can't count on anyone else. I should have just done it myself.' Then the silent treatment and the ice wall. This was NORMAL to me. Normal! I feel like I was the most recent in my family line to use my power to communicate. To say I feel much lighter is an understatement!"

Both of these situations needed a good power chakra clearing to clean out this old energy. You can do the same to tap into the energy of your 3rd chakra. (Spoiler: there's a powerful clearing for you in the exercises at the end of this chapter.) It's easy to do and your energy responds very quickly.

SHIFTING FROM THE OLD TO NEW ENERGY OF PARENTING

The shift from old energy to new energy also affects parenting. The experience of dominance and control played out in the old model as, "Do what I say because I am the parent," and "Children should be seen and not heard." More and more parents are abandoning fear, guilt, and shame-based parenting approaches for more conscious ones. I have seen this firsthand with my work as a parenting expert and coach with my *Child Whisperer* book and podcast. The old authoritarian model doesn't feel right to them and they have been drawn to *The Child Whisperer* body of work because they are looking for new, healthy parenting strategies. Parents of today are open to learning more about their children and how to honor, teach, and guide. When discipline is necessary, they discipline more from their heart chakra than from their power chakra.

Interestingly, the energy of parenting began to shift when fathers started to attend their children's births. This created a partnership energy that continued to grow in shifting the rigid parental roles of Mom being the primary childcare giver and Dad being the breadwinner. More women pursuing professional roles was met with concern that it would take both parents out of the home, when it actually brought more fathers back into the home to create a joint parenting effort.

My children's parenting philosophy and practice in their 20s and 30s, looks completely different from my husband's and mine during the same age in our parenting lives. My children and their spouses are partners with every aspect of their parenting. They have dismissed traditional male and female roles and work in partnership in taking care of household and domestic needs and all parenting responsibilities. This is just one huge benefit coming from the shift of the old energy of the power chakra. There are many, many more!

Exercises to Strengthen the
New Energy of the Power Chakra

Use any and all of the following exercises to help you ground the new energy of the power chakra into your personal energy system. You can use them as frequently as you find supportive.

Clearing the Old Energy of the Power Chakra

Sit in a comfortable position with your arms and legs uncrossed. Take three deep, relaxing, cleansing breaths. Holding your hand in the space of your power chakra, rotate your hand counterclockwise as if you are unwinding the old energy. Repeat the following as you rotate your hand:

- Even though I have given my power away, I am ready to claim it
- I am releasing the belief that other people have more power than I do
- I am releasing the pattern of giving my power away
- I am releasing the pattern of pleasing others
- I am releasing the belief that I don't have any power
- I am releasing the belief that I have to please others to get my needs met
- I am releasing the belief that I will hurt people's feelings if I am not agreeable
- I am releasing the belief that I need to go along with the crowd so I don't draw attention to myself
- I am releasing the belief I need to just go along with it to avoid an upset
- I am releasing the belief that what I want doesn't matter, my needs are not important

- I am no longer letting others steal my power

Take three deep breaths and let go of all of this old energy. Now rotate your hand in the clockwise direction as though you are turning on the power chakra. While rotating your hand think or speak the following:

- I am connected to my own authentic power
- I am powerful and I am using my power to bless my life and the lives of others
- I am grateful this new energy is helping me create love and partnership
- I am grateful this new energy is attracting to me what is timely and correct
- I am grateful this new energy is helping bring my life purpose into formation
- I am recognized for my power of making a difference
- Rest your hand, take a deep breath, and breathe in this new energy. Sit still as though you are sitting in your power. Feel it, sense it, thank it, and bask in the energy of your personal power.

Committing to a Personal Challenge You Believe is Hard!

Years ago, my husband and I challenged ourselves to run a marathon. We honestly believed we could not do it, and that's why we challenged ourselves to do it anyway! We not only ran that first marathon, we went on to run 15 more!

What is something that calls to you that you believe you cannot do? That is how the marathon showed up for us. It was like the Universe was enrolling us to help us see how much power we had.

Create a support system that will help you succeed. We joined a marathon coaching program for first-time marathon runners. My running coach even ran the last mile of the marathon with us!

Side note: Running our marathon together helped create more partnership in our relationship. We both had the benefits of it activating our power chakra, which then activated our relationship.

Strengthening Your Core

Strengthening your core energy will strengthen your power chakra. Strengthening your entire core physically strengthens the muscles that support the entire body in everyday movements, reduces back pain, and improves posture. When you have a strong core, you have better posture. When you have better posture, you have increased self-confidence. Numerous exercises can help you strengthen your core, including the well-known plank pose. If you do not know how to do a plank pose, just google "plank pose" and you can easily learn from written instructions and videos how to do this power chakra enhancing exercise.

Claiming Your Power With Essential Oils

Massage a few drops of essential oils on the location of the 3rd chakra on the upper abdomen, just below the sternum. Carol Tuttle Healing Oils are custom blends that support you with specific healing goals. These oil blends can be used to activate and strengthen the power chakra in the following ways:

- **I am confident:** This oil will assist you in acting on what is correct and timely in your life, with unwavering confidence.
- **I am fit:** This oil infuses you with the motivation to take care of your body, to take necessary action to let go of excess weight, and follow through on a fitness plan that supports your body's well-being.

What key thing did you learn from this section?

Use this space to make notes. Write down questions and insights you had while reading this section.

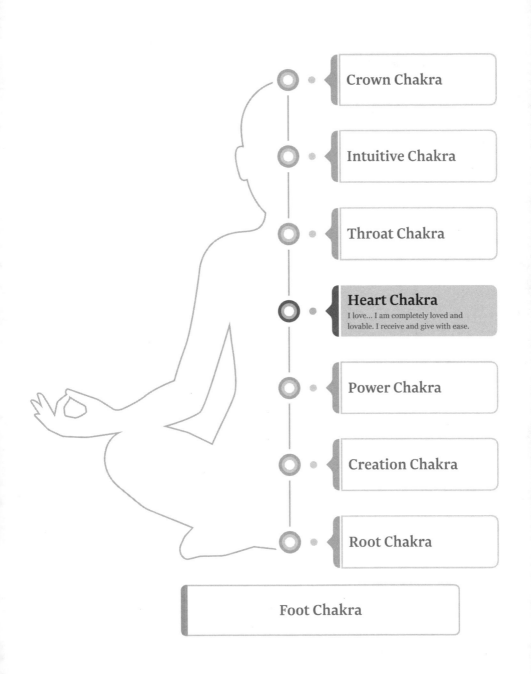

Crown Chakra

Intuitive Chakra

Throat Chakra

Heart Chakra
I love... I am completely loved and
lovable. I receive and give with ease.

Power Chakra

Creation Chakra

Root Chakra

Foot Chakra

Step 4: Opening Your Heart

• • • • • • •

4th Chakra—The Heart Chakra

Location:	The middle of the chest and space between the shoulder blades.
Yin/Yang Flow:	Yin and yang energy, with the energy moving into us for us to receive first and then outward as we give.
Universal Color:	Green
Associated Organs and Body Parts:	Heart and lungs. Imbalances in this chakra can manifest as various issues of the heart and lungs, such as heart attack, asthma, breast issues, or upper back problems.
Function:	Energetically connecting us with our emotions, compassion, gratitude, universal love and peace, and the new energy of money.
Old Energy:	I have to protect my heart to keep it from getting hurt.
New Energy:	As I open my heart, my life heals and I thrive.
If Closed:	Your feelings get hurt easily. You feel you have to keep your heart protected or closed so you don't trigger repressed and hurt feelings from your childhood. You don't easily feel happy and it's a challenge feeling joyful for very long. You lead with your head more often than your heart.
If Open:	You feel joyful for no apparent reason. You easily attract love and support in your life. Just as you abundantly receive, you easily and freely give. You feel a heartfelt sense of gratitude for how wonderful your life is. You appreciate others and feel compassion for yourself and others without feeling sorry for anyone.
Affirmation:	I love. I am completely loved and lovable. I receive and give with ease.
Carol Tuttle Healing Oil Blends:	I am joyful I am nurtured I am rich

The fourth step in awakening brings us into the heart chakra energy. The heart chakra is the bridge that connects the lower three chakras to the upper three chakras—connecting the outer world and the inner world.

Working with your heart chakra may be the very first place you start with your chakra work. If you are stuck in the old survival energy of the lower three chakras, activating the new energy of your heart chakra will awaken you faster than working with any other single chakra. In other words, you may be stuck in fear or live what I call a "prevention" lifestyle (trying to prevent bad things from happening, rather than creating what you want). If that's the case for you, activating your heart energy will open your connection to your higher chakras where the energy of love, truth, higher knowing, and divine support can all feed you on a daily basis. The energy of the upper three chakras (our voice, our insight, and our divine connection) move through the bridge of the heart chakra to feed the lower chakras and turn on the new energy that is available to us in those energy centers.

Before I opened my heart chakra, I lived my life as a victim. I was stuck in the pain of the unhealed wounds of my childhood. When my chakra system was activated way back in 1991, my heart opened. I started to find my voice and wrote my first book in 1993. My intuition was energized and I started to develop the psychic and empathic abilities I have today. My spiritual eyes were opened to the potential of healing that I could achieve. Activating my heart chakra did not remove all the old wounds, but it helped balance my perspective and started me on my path of awakening to fully and completely heal those wounds. Your heart is powerful. It's worthwhile to consider the common misunderstanding about this powerful energy center and what it can support us with.

THE OLD ENERGY OF THE HEART CHAKRA

I am sure you have heard this phrase or even spoken it: "I am broken-hearted." If we identify the feelings this phrase represents, we could say it is a way for us to express our sadness, disappointment, anger, or disgust. We can honestly have those feelings, but your heart energy cannot be broken. It can be shut down, blocked, frozen, dormant, muddled with old issues, leaky, weak, or hanging outside your energy field, but it can't be broken. It can be dysfunctional, but it is always intact. It would be more appropriate to say, "I have a dysfunctional heart chakra!"

The heart chakra is responsible for our emotions, and is the center of our energy for happiness, love, sadness, and anger. Along with being the center of our emotional experience, your heart chakra is the space in which your "inner child" resides when it is healthy and balanced.

Your inner child is a metaphorical reference to a part of you that experiences the wonder and joy of this world with love and appreciation, just as you were meant to experience it in your childhood! We all carry some degree of unmet emotional needs and childhood wounding, due to trauma, lack, or the dysfunction of our parents and the generations that preceded them. When you are carrying around repressed childhood emotions, your inner child cannot reside whole and complete in your heart chakra. That part of you is energetically "pulled out" and hanging out somewhere in your auric field or personal energy system. When it's too scary to feel your feelings, you have to keep your heart closed or shut off to some degree. You pay a price for closing off, though. When you get emotionally triggered, you feel those repressed feelings in a magnified manner, and they get the best of you. You can lose your emotional balance and overreact or retreat, make choices that are not a reflection of an emotionally mature person, or struggle to deal with present-day situations that appear to be hurtful. Really, the current event is just tapping into the unresolved hurts of the past.

Based on how our parents modeled handling or repressing emotions, we may also run a psychological reversal in our beliefs about feelings. Many people were taught that feelings should be avoided and put aside. As one of my clients shared:

> *"Mankind has devalued feelings. Feelings are worthless, feelings must be controlled, put away, denied, covered up. We must not feel them if they are bad; we should only feel good feelings. Painful, suffering feelings are to be hidden, ignored; they are stupid; they cause weakness. We have been taught that the intellect is of great value; it is of great worth—show it off, take care of it teach it, nurture it, fill it up, be proud of it, use it to control your feelings."*

When your heart chakra is whole and healthy, you are an emotionally open and balanced person who deals with the issues of life with emotional maturity and awareness. You realize you cannot be "hurt" by others, and that you are responsible for your own feelings and happiness. You also mature to an emotional state of feeling good for no reason!

THE NEW ENERGY OF THE HEART CHAKRA

The new energy of the heart chakra is FEELING! Allow yourself to feel all your feelings, bring up and heal the repressed, unpleasant, and uncomfortable feelings of your past, feel the feelings that are stirred in the present situations of your life, and keep your heart open to both receiving and giving love. As you heal the repressed feelings of your past, you are freed to feel powerful feelings of love, joy, happiness, and fulfillment in the present.

The following are indicators that the new energy of the 4th chakra is getting activated for you. Which of these have you experienced?

- Your emotions are easily triggered by your children or spouse.
- You recognize and feel uncomfortable about media that involves cruelty towards people as part of the storyline.
- You notice that social media brings out a judgmental side of you.
- You are more aware of your poor choices and want to make changes for the better.
- You feel moved to give back and help out in some way in life to make the world a better place.
- You want to have more money because you want the freedom to do good with it and help others in need.

FEELING GOOD FOR NO REASON

When your heart chakra is healthy and open, you have the experience on a regular basis of feeling good for no reason! I remember my first experiences with this. I would be driving along in my car and just happen to notice how amazing and joyful I felt, and I could not place any reason for it. In the old energy of the heart chakra, we believe that we need outside experiences to provoke a state of joy and happiness. That is what all addictions are connected to—needing something to help us feel better or drown out or mask the negative feelings. Tapping into the new energy of the heart chakra and fully opening our hearts helps us heal every disabling and compromising condition we are meant to heal. Every time I noticed these states of, "feeling good for no reason," I put my attention on it, took deep breaths while I tapped on my chest (my heart chakra center) 5-6 times, while repeating, "I am feeling good for no reason and it is normal." Doing this helps ground the energy so that it can become the new normal of your experience.

HOW TO OPEN YOUR HEART

Your heart chakra energy is naturally opening and expanding with the new energy available to us. Allow yourself to feel all of your feelings. This is an important choice to further support the opening and expansion of this energy. As I mentioned before, a common false belief is that the denial of feelings builds inner strength. The truth is, self-honesty and the appropriate expression of feelings takes strength and courage and expands your heart.

Choosing to feel all of your feelings means willingness to feel any repressed or negative feelings from your past that you have stuffed away. Feeling negative feelings is obviously uncomfortable. Yet, when you do, you are supporting your energy system in learning how to let this energy go. You no longer have to hang onto it. Repressed emotions have to be accounted for somehow, and if you do not allow them to come forward, your body takes on the energy, which eventually breaks the body down. The negative or "bad" emotions are really "healing" emotions. Shame, worthlessness, and powerlessness are only feelings. They are not who you are. Allowing yourself to experience all your feelings will enable you to find out who you really are and will generate feelings of love, joy, peace, happiness, enthusiasm, and other pleasurable emotions.

The children of today are a great example to us of feeling their feelings in the moment—both the positive ones we enjoy having them express, and the negative ones that are very uncomfortable for us to experience them expressing.

If you have younger children who were born after the year 2000, they are cut from a different energetic cloth than you. Energetically, they are built differently. The primary difference between you and them is that they cannot shut themselves down emotionally like we could. They can only be their true selves. If they are happy, they feel it and express it. If they are angry, they feel it and express it. If they are sad, they feel it and express it. And often they express it in a magnified way. This can catch today's parents off guard, as they were not necessarily raised by parents who showed them how to support a child who is expressing powerful emotions. The common strategy of parents in past generations was to shut down feelings and silence them. Parents of today are having to navigate a more emotionally charged parenting experience, as children are willing to feel!

If you ever attempted to quiet your children's emotional expression, they will just counter your effort by expressing their feelings more fully and intensely. You will know they are feeling. And when your child feels the feelings that you have not yet given yourself permission to feel, those feelings get stirred up for you and provoke feelings to come to the surface. Because we don't want to feel those uncomfortable feelings, we often try to silence or find a fix for our children's feelings. That way, we don't have to feel ours. But they aren't willing to be silenced!

In some cases, due to lack of emotional wisdom or understanding of the emotional energy body, parents turn to medicine to find out what is wrong with their child. Why are they so extreme in expressing themselves? As a result, there has been an increase in diagnostic categories in the area of emotional and mental health issues for children. Could we be pathologizing normal childhood behavior because we don't understand what a more conscious, fully expressive human looks like as a child? Are we compromising a child's genius under the illusion of a behavioral disorder?

You may have heard of Marie Kondo who created the popular organizing method called Konmari. As a child, she had an obsession with organizing and creating structure in her living environment.[30] By most parents' standards, her interest in this as a child would be seen as abnormal and extreme. What if Marie had been diagnosed with OCD, or sensory processing disorder when she was young? Would she have been free to develop her unique qualities and interests into a world-wide sensation?

Being emotionally triggered by your children can actually be a favorable opportunity for you to help you open your heart. The next time you experience your child expressing strong feelings, join it, rather than try and change it. That doesn't mean you have to throw a tantrum alongside your child. You just need to turn within and notice what is coming up for you. Take a deep breath and say to yourself, "This little person is here to help me open my heart and feel all of my feelings. I accept that." Once you have given yourself permission to feel, you won't be so eager to silence your child's feelings and will be more motivated to address the issue that is provoking your child.

As you embrace what you are feeling, you are letting that energy expand your heart. When you feel moved to tears, let the tears and the energy come. When you feel moved to anger, feel that anger and write out what that anger is really about from your past. When you feel joy, celebrate that joy and breathe in the fullness of it. You are a feeling being. Your heart chakra is ready to support you in feeling ALL of your feelings whenever they share themselves with you.

CHANGE OF HEART

When we open our heart energy, we have the power to open other people's heart energy, too. This happens as we send the vibration of our
heart energy out into the world and it energetically opens and activates
others. We have the power to open the hearts of our intimate partners,
without even saying a word.

The following story is about a client I worked with years ago. She had
come to me to learn how she could help her husband open his heart to
accept and love their daughter who had recently shared with my client
that she was gay. They had not told the father, as the daughter feared
he would reject and shame her. Her story will give you pointers on how
to approach potentially painful conversations:

> "When I found out my daughter was gay, I did not have any issues
> with it. My concern was for her and the difficult life she might
> have, due to people not accepting her. I was also worried about
> how her dad would react. She had heard her dad make gay slurs.
> I knew my daughter well enough to know that if her dad was in
> any way shaming in how he reacted, there could be irreparable
> damage and my daughter would estrange herself. I knew the stress
> in my heart and in my daughter's, so I sought Carol out to help us.
>
> Carol tuned into my husband's heart chakra and shared that it
> had the energy of being strangled. She saw ropes around the image
> of a heart. In a visualization, I removed all the rope that was
> strangling his heart. I saw his heart puff up and start pumping
> and radiating.

She also taught me to start doing figure 8's between me, my husband, and our daughter. I would imagine the three of us standing in a circle and connect my heart with my husband's, then his heart to our daughter's, and her heart connecting back to mine.

Our daughter asked to meet with both of us for lunch. She wanted to talk to her dad and share with him that she was gay. We decided that it would be beneficial for me to speak with him first to give him time to process his feelings first.

I grew up in a family where I didn't have a voice. Children were expected to follow orders without question, and when you didn't, you were punished. I had been working on opening my throat chakra to speak my truth. I had a great opportunity to practice this when I shared with my husband that our daughter is gay. I shared with him that I was going to love and support her and hoped he could do the same. His response surprised me. He shared that he had forgotten how to be happy and that he wanted to be happy again so he could show up for her. He knew he needed to look inside himself for real happiness. I was stunned. Could the work Carol had taught me to do with opening my husband's heart energy and connecting it to my daughter's have prompted this? I am willing to believe it did.

We met with our daughter. There were a lot tears shed and feelings shared and we all left with hope that we could learn how to navigate this new experience with each other and open our hearts to love each other no matter what."

The next time you have a relationship conflict or a challenging conversation ahead of you, try the technique that this client used. Connect your hearts energetically with figure 8s. The more you strengthen and activate your own heart chakra, the more you can influence others for good.

Remember, any changes that you influence in your relationship begin with yourself—not by changing anyone else. Do your own work to open your heart chakra and then allow the effects of that work to come into your life. Don't get discouraged if it takes some time. This experience by a member of The Carol Tuttle Healing Center shows you how change can come about in a relationship by focusing on your own healing:

> *"I'm so thrilled to share that since I have been working on healing my heart, my husband told me that he has noticed such an amazing shift in me that he is going to start to work on past issues in his life that he realizes need to be healed. He has always been supportive of me pursuing resources to help me heal, but despite generations of emotional wounding on his side of the family he has been reluctant to seek any kind of therapy or assistance until now. Just yesterday he said that he has been so impressed with the healing and stability of my emotional and mental health he is going to start one of Carol's healing plans this week. Decades and decades of emotional trauma and wounding are stopping now...I am overwhelmed with gratitude and have such hope for our future."*

Your heart energy is one of the most powerful tools you have to effect a positive change in other people—more powerful than your voice. Is your heart open? Are you allowing yourself to feel all of your feelings?

Is your heart chakra blocked by any forgiveness that needs to happen toward yourself or others?

THE OPEN HEART IS A FORGIVING HEART

I've come to believe that embodied in the heart chakra energy is the energy and feeling of forgiveness. Forgiveness is not a mental act, but a byproduct of emotionally letting go of the pain, hurt, and wounds that have been carried throughout your life. When this emotional shift takes place, your heart chakra opens the energy of forgiveness in you and your mind is opened up to a higher awareness. You become aware that those who hurt you were also hurt. You see that we are all affected by the misdeeds and abusive acts passed on by the generations that preceded us. You understand that your soul was willing to step into that chain of generational events and stop the wounding.

Forgiveness is a tricky experience. Too often, it feels like it benefits the person in the wrong and leaves us feeling like the unaccounted for victim again. That depends on which part of you is doing the forgiving. One of the most profound insights I came to in my personal healing work was that my inner child didn't need to forgive anyone! That part of me took on all the pain and suffering as a powerless child, and cannot be expected to understand the workings of our higher self where true forgiveness originates. Letting my inner child off the forgiveness hook was incredibly healing. Telling that part of me that had been abused, raped, and mistreated that she did not need to forgive made it easy for me to forgive!

As you forgive those who hurt you, you give your freedom back to yourself. You release yourself from the stories of past generations and no longer energetically hold that as your own story. You have the memories of your hurts in your logical mind, yet you no longer carry the side effects as something that limits and compromises you.

Forgiveness is an act of an open heart, not a mental decision. You cannot plan it or force it. Anything that does not come from your heart is just the mind's attempt to act like you are forgiving. Forgiving will not lead to healing; healing opens our heart to forgiving. In her book, *Toxic Parents,* Susan Forward helps us understand the folly of mental forgiveness, rather than heart-centered forgiveness, "One of the most dangerous things about forgiveness too soon, is that it undercuts your ability to let go of your pent-up emotions. How can you acknowledge your anger if you have already forgiven? Responsibility can go only one of two places: outward onto the person who has hurt you, or inward, into yourself. Someone's got to be accountable. So you may forgive your offender and end up hating yourself all the more in exchange."[31]

If you are involved in a religious community, the pressure of needing to forgive can be great, especially when it is encouraged by family, friends, and religious leaders. In an attempt to be helpful you may hear things like, "Why can't you get on with your life? You're just hurting yourself by not forgiving. Can't you just forgive and forget? Why can't you let it go?" Trust that your heart chakra has forgiveness on the agenda as part of your healing. Intellectual forgiveness is not the goal.

In the years that I was estranged from my family, I knew I was not ready to forgive my father. Yet I knew that someday I would. I allowed myself to move through my healing process without feeling forced to forgive on any timeline. Then, one day in the mid-90s, I was watching the *Oprah Winfrey Show.* For several years prior, Oprah had been sharing her story of childhood abuse and regularly hosted shows to support her audience in their own healing. At the end of one of those shows, in a close-up shot, Oprah appealed to her viewing audience to open their hearts to forgive. She shared from her heart how she had come to forgive her offenders and how it had blessed her life. She shared that we were only hurting ourselves by not forgiving. I felt my heart open that afternoon and was brought to tears. Oprah's heart opened my heart that day. Within the next few days, I wrote a sincere, heartfelt letter to my dad and told him I wanted to renew my relationship with him. I had one condition: that we both let the past go and commit to moving forward. My dad responded and asked to come visit me within the month. It wasn't easy agreeing to this and choosing to see my dad. I still had a lot of healing to do. But my heart was telling me this is correct, so I followed my heart, not my mind.

I remember the day my dad came to my home and how nervous I was. I had not seen him in close to five years. That day involved a lot of tears and awkwardness, but I broke the chain of three generations of parent/child estrangement that day, thanks to following my heart. My relationship with my father from then on out was never ideal or amazing. But it was free of past hurts. I was able to be the adult child and have adult boundaries and an adult relationship with my father and he was who he was. I learned from this experience that our heart moves us to forgiveness when the time is right and that forgiveness is not an act that the mind is in charge of.

My father passed away in 2018 at the age of 90. I saw him five days before his passing. He was still wrestling with life and his inner demons. He was a narcissist who could barely see beyond his own pain and anguish. I knew not to expect much from him, as that just led me into emotional disappointment. I didn't know he was going to pass, so my visit was brief as we exchanged polite superficial thoughts with each other. The day that I learned that he had passed, the first thing I grieved and allowed myself to feel was how sad I was that I didn't get the last visit experience with my dad. He just wasn't emotionally and mentally healthy enough of a human to give me that. I felt the sadness of never having "that" father who sat you on his knee, who you ran to with eagerness as a kid, who was there for you as an adult to help you and guide you, who was your friend and role model. That never happened in my life. I grieved the loss of not having a father who really knew me and deeply cared about me. Instead, I had a father who abused me and was often rude to me. I also allowed myself to feel the gratitude I had for being in a place of clarity and forgiveness about my story with my dad. No resentments, no regrets, no anger, just peace. I felt an overwhelming love and appreciation for the role my dad played for me. Because if it weren't for my dad, I think I would have gone into high-end real estate, rather than the work of helping others heal! I know how much my dad loves me now that he is released from the emotional and mental impairments he acquired from his own childhood wounding. I am grateful I followed my heart and forgave my father when I did, as the years to follow allowed me to fully heal from my childhood wounds so that when my father passed I was free to feel the love he truly has for me.

My heart led me to reconcile my relationship with my dad. That may or may not be the experience that is correct for you. As you follow your heart, it will guide you in what (and when) is correct for you. Remember, what forgiveness looks like for you is written in the agenda of your heart chakra. You came with that intact. It is a natural by-product of healing. Until the experience of forgiveness presents itself, keep healing.

THE NEW ENERGY OF MONEY

This may seem like an odd chapter to talk about money, since the common chakra teaching is that money is connected to our root chakra. This is true, but in the new energy of our chakras in today's world, money has been given an upgrade.

Money wants to be used to make a difference in the world, not to be used for control and domination. Consider the possibility that the economic collapses that societies move through could be connected to a collapse of the old energy of money.

Money wants to flow to you as you follow your heart's passion and use the energy of your lower three chakras to stand for what you want, get on your life path, express your creativity in your work, and take inspired action to bring it into manifestation. Then the money shows up for you! You believe you can do what you love and the money will follow.

Numerous examples show that money has taken on a heartfelt energy in today's culture. Platforms like Kiva, KickStarter, and Go Fund Me all allow peer-to-peer support in helping people build their businesses, pursue their dreams, or help pay for medical expenses without involving large banks or financial institutions. This is the energy of the heart at work—opening our hearts so that we open our pocketbooks to help others. The sharing economy was birthed from the heart chakra energy. The largest ride-sharing network in the world does not even own an automobile and the largest travel accommodation network does not even own a hotel! Platforms like Uber and Airbnb allow us to share with our peers without the bulk of the money going to a large organization.

If you are still experiencing money as a struggle, you are connecting to the old energy of money in your root chakra. If you are experiencing money as a tool you are grateful for and know you will always have an ample supply, you are now connected to money from your heart chakra.

HOW TO UPGRADE THE ENERGY OF MONEY

The first step in upgrading the energy of money is changing how you think about money. This is where prevention thinking vs creation thinking is very powerful.

- Do you think more about trying not to run out of money or do you think about creating more money and how money will always be there for you?
- Do you tell yourself you can't afford things and then feel bad about not having the same opportunities as others, or do you believe that you can have the opportunities and things you want?
- Do you feel powerless about money or do you feel you are the one in charge of your experience with money?
- Can you say, "I love money and money loves me," without feeling shameful, worldly or greedy?

I have taught for several decades that money is neither good nor bad. It is a neutral energy that we project our energy and story onto. Our story creates our money experience for us. Money is powerless. We endow it with the power it has in our lives through our thoughts and feelings about it. Most people have never cleared out the old energy of money from their root chakra that they inherited from their parents. All the stories of struggle with money, the expressions spoken about money in your childhood, are all energetically imprinted in your root chakra. When you clear that old energy out, you free up the energy of money to activate in your heart chakra, so you can create your modern-day experience of affluence and ease with money.

To start growing the new energy of money in your heart, look at money as an energy of appreciation and gratitude that is exchanged for services and experiences you receive.

I have taught principles about the new energy of money in depth for several decades now. I have numerous online resources, both free and paid, that help you clear out the old energy of money from your root chakra and then help you activate the new energy of money in your heart chakra. To start, use the Visualization to Upgrade the Energy of Money in the next section, at the end of this chapter.

Exercises to Activate the New Energy of the Heart Chakra

Use any and all of the following exercises to help you ground the new energy of the heart chakra into your personal energy system. You can use them as frequently as you find supportive.

Showing Yourself Some Kindness
What is something you've been wanting to do for yourself that you keep putting off? Decide right now when you are going to do it and put it in your schedule. If arrangements need to be made, take time today to make them. Doing something kind for yourself on a regular basis nurtures and opens your heart chakra.

Praising Everyone You Meet for a Day
There is something special about everyone and you can see what that is when you set the intention to do so. Most people feel undervalued. Praising others acknowledges their worth and value and gives them a boost of self-confidence. Hold the affirmation in your heart: "I easily

see the good in others and praise them authentically." Give yourself the assignment to find something wonderful about every person you interact with today—then tell it to them. Sharing this positive energy strengthens your heart chakra.

Making Heart Connections

To create stronger heart connections with those you love, draw an image of yourself as a stick figure on a sketch pad. Draw the image in a stick figure of the people you want to have a stronger heart connection with in a circle with you. Draw figure 8's between your heart energy and theirs.

Writing Yourself a Love Letter

What can you honestly say you love about yourself? Share your love and appreciation with yourself in a love letter to you, signed by you.

Reflecting in the Mirror

When you look in the mirror, think a loving thought about yourself rather than a critical or shaming thought.

Going on a Complaint-Free Diet

For an entire week, stop complaining and replace your complaints with thoughts and expressions of gratitude. Gratitude feeds the heart and then your heart energy becomes more powerful as it radiates out into the world to attract more experiences for which you will feel grateful for. (For more info on this idea, you can look into the book, *A Complaint Free World*, by Will Bowen.[32])

Visualization to Upgrade the Energy of Money

1. Close your eyes and tune into your heart chakra, placing your hand on your chest. You are going to create a new reference to the new energy of money, by asking yourself a few questions.

2. If the new energy of money had a new image, what would it look like? Bring that picture to mind. What does it look like?

3. Imagine the new energy of money had a sound. What would the sound be? Imagine you can hear it as you tune into it. What does it sound like?

4. What would the new energy of money smell like if it had a smell? Imagine you can smell it. Imagine you have a handful of money that you are holding close to your nose and take a deep breaths in. What does it smell like?

5. What does the new energy of money feel like? Imagine you are stroking the money with your finger. How does it feel?

6. If the new energy of money had a taste what would it taste like? Imagine you can put that taste on your tongue. What is the taste?

7. Visualize taking the sight, sound, smell, feel, and taste of the new energy of money and place it in your heart chakra.

8. Now imagine something you desire, something that would make your heart happy that you could use money for to acquire or accomplish in your life. Tell the new energy of money what you want. Draw sideways figure 8's out from your heart to what you desire. Do this 7-8 times.

9. Money is a currency that now flows to your heart in abundance. Thank the energy of money for flowing to you so effortlessly. Place your hands on your heart chakra, the center of your chest, and repeat out loud, "I love money and money loves me. I am grateful." Take a deep breath and gently open your eyes.

Opening Your Heart With Essential Oils

Massage a few drops of essential oils on the location of the 4th chakra on the center of your chest, while you take deep, cleansing breaths. Carol Tuttle Healing Oils are custom blends that support you with specific healing goals. These oil blends can be used to activate and strengthen the heart chakra in the following ways:

- **I am joyful:** This oil will assist you in opening your heart to stream the natural energy of joy that is available to all of us.
- **I am nurtured:** This oil will assist you in healing past emotional wounding from childhood, so you can feel loved and nurtured, which automatically attracts more love and nurturing from others.
- **I am rich:** This oil assists you in connecting your heart energy with the energy of money, so you can do what you love and money will flow and accumulate to support you.

What key thing did you learn from this section?

Use this space to make notes. Write down questions and insights you had while reading this section.

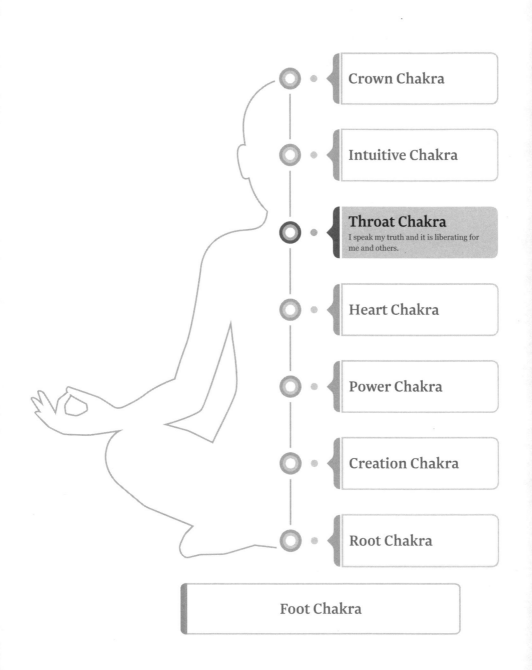

Crown Chakra

Intuitive Chakra

Throat Chakra
I speak my truth and it is liberating for me and others.

Heart Chakra

Power Chakra

Creation Chakra

Root Chakra

Foot Chakra

Step 5: Speaking Your Truth

• • • • • • •

5th Chakra—The Throat Chakra

Location:	The larynx or middle of the throat on both sides of the neck.
Yin/Yang Flow:	Yang energy flowing outward as we express ourselves with our voice.
Universal Color:	Blue
Associated Organs and Body Parts:	Throat, thyroid, vocal chords, jaw, mouth, and neck. Imbalance in this chakra can manifest physically as sore throats, dental issues, thyroid problems, TMJ or neck pain.
Function:	Energetically connecting us to our true voice so we can speak our truth with confidence and ease.
Old Energy:	I have to deny what is true for me and go along with what is best for the group.
New Energy:	I speak what is true for me with confidence and I am supported.
If Closed:	You are afraid to speak up and say what you want or feel. You worry that you will be challenged, judged, or chastised. You get sore throats often or feel as if your throat is blocked.
If Open:	You are comfortable speaking what is true for you in a civil and polite manner. You experience others listening and hearing you. You experience being heard and honored for your truth.
Affirmation:	I speak my truth and it is liberating for me and others.
Carol Tuttle Healing Oil Blends:	I am connected I am confident

The fourth step in awakening brings us into the throat chakra energy. The throat chakra has an interesting history. In ancient societies, only a few had a voice to influence humanity. The pendulum has now swung to the other extreme, so that now the masses have the chance to have a voice. It's interesting to live at a time when social media and other platforms make it easy for people to use their voice. The question is: Are we using this opportunity in alignment with the new energy of the throat chakra? Or are we still playing in the old energy and just adding a lot of noise to the world? Let's take a look at this present and powerful energy center that is filling our airwaves to the brim!

THE OLD ENERGY OF THE THROAT CHAKRA

In ancient times, the few who sat at the top of the hierarchy, running governments or religions, were the only ones who were allowed to have a public voice. The people of the communities they ruled were forced to keep silent or have their lives threatened. In the United States' not-too-distant past, even within the span of my lifetime, speaking one's truth in certain parts of the country could be a risk to their life, due to racial prejudice.

However, as you look through history, you can see that the throat chakra never went quiet from its earliest beginnings. Even in the face of risk, a continuous stream of people have tried to make their voice heard, from centuries ago to modern times. In some areas of the world, speaking up still has a risk of personal safety, but the new energy of the throat chakra is inspiring people to speak up anyway. In locations where speaking your truth does not carry the risk of losing your life, you may risk being bullied or harassed online. If you have felt blocked in speaking your truth publicly, my personal experience can help you to move forward and activate this chakra with confidence. I share the following story to show you how much the energy has opened to support us in speaking our truth.

I made a choice in the year 2000 to go online and share my truth. My first book that became available online was published in the year 2000, *Remembering Wholeness*. I launched my first website that same year. At that time, the energy was just beginning to open and would expand more significantly over the next 20 years than we have ever experienced on this planet.

When I was prompted to write *Remembering Wholeness*, I felt hesitant. I knew I would be writing about experiences and beliefs I had formed that were true for me as a result of the nine years of healing I had done using the tools of energy therapy. I also had six years of successful energy therapy practice under my belt and I was a firm believer that, due to what I had learned and applied in my life, my life had been saved and my family kept intact. I knew that the Spirit and God had led me to these resources and the answers I had found, and I wanted to share them with others.

I hesitated because I knew that my writing about this would be considered blasphemy by some in my religious community and refuted and judged as inappropriate by many. I could foresee that some would say that I had no right to share what I would share and that it was dangerous to even read my book. I also knew that thousands of people's lives would be blessed and helped by the teachings I would share in *Remembering Wholeness*. If you have not yet read this powerful book, in a nutshell, I was one of the first authors to publish a book that shared Christian truths with metaphysical philosophies and practices. Could I dare write that Christ was actually a healer of the quantum field of energy? Could I write about being psychic and then within a few pages, make reference to Christ's life? I knew I was going to push a lot of buttons. With my psychic gift of fore-knowing, I was shown that I would have to go through an experience of being judged by leaders from my church at a high level. I wrote the first edition of *Remembering Wholeness* in 2000. The internet was new and yet to be integrated into our daily lives, so it wasn't until 2004 that what I had seen started to play out.

Out of the blue one day, my husband and I received an invitation to meet with our local church leaders. We were not suspicious of anything, so we eagerly agreed to meet. We had no idea that we were being invited in to be questioned and challenged on what I taught in *Remembering Wholeness*. This was not a friendly, we'd-like-to-learn-more meeting. Instead, it was a grueling three-hour encounter. The local leaders of my church shared with me that they had been assigned to investigate if I was an apostate or not. Before I even got to the meeting, I had already been judged as being an apostate of my own faith.

During those three hours, I had an interesting and powerful experience occur. I felt as though I was held in the arms of a higher power that helped me maintain my dignity and composure without retaliation or self-defense. My husband stood by me and shared his belief in me and in what I was doing.

At the end of the three hours, the leader of my congregation said to me, "If God were to tell you today you have to stop teaching what you are teaching, would you agree?" My answer came from a higher part of myself, as I shared, "I don't know. I would have to pray to know for sure who is asking, you or God, so I do not feel like I need to answer that today."

My church leaders had the authority to decide my standing in the congregation—whether I would be welcome or not. No decisions were made that day by my leaders. Instead they wanted me to go home and pray to get an answer for myself about what I should do. I said I would, and they agreed to meet again.

I took this matter seriously. I also had the ability to put it into perspective. I know I have a gift of receiving insights and universal truths ahead of their time. Thirteen years earlier, I had attended a 12-step group. My local church leaders frowned on that. But 10 years later, my same church organized 12-step programs within their own ranks! I knew that what I had written in *Remembering Wholeness* was ahead of its time. I was teaching about the laws of creation, more popularly referred to as the law of attraction, at least five years before Oprah made it a "thing!"

I went home that day and I got on my knees and prayed. I remember saying to God, "Have I been deceived? Because if I have, I am willing to accept that and remedy the situation. I will do what you want me to do. If I have been led by the spirit and done what you have wanted me to do, God, and written what you have wanted me to write in *Remembering Wholeness*, I will stand by that as my truth and accept whatever course this takes, even if it leads to being excommunicated." I humbled myself, with willingness to do what was correct for me. Only moments after I boldly spoke that prayer, the spirit overcame me and I heard God say to me, "Good for you, Carol. That is all I needed to know, that you were not going to be swayed by fear. I can give you more. I have led you and guided you on this path and I will continue to do so."

Over the next several months, I attended meetings and follow-up visits with my church leaders to work through this. I continued to pray for strength to stay clear, composed, and civil in my manner, to listen and understand. I attempted to explain to my church leader that I was a self-help author and I wasn't interested in influencing people's religious experiences, that I was sharing what was truth for me, and if it helped another person, I was grateful. His biggest fear was that I was getting a "following."

About four months into this experience, he invited my husband to meet with him alone. Jon and I thought maybe he was concerned that Jon couldn't speak his truth and share his opinion in my presence. Since the issue about having a "following" had presented itself, I felt prompted to have Jon share with him a part of a blessing that I had received when I was 16 years old. In my religious community, it's a common practice to receive a blessing during your youth from a designated authority who served in that role to help provide God's guidance to you in your life. In my blessing, the phrase that was shared with me was, "You will have a following of good people who will want to learn more from you. You have a gift of discernment, use that gift to bless the lives of many and do good works on the earth." That blessing was given in 1974, 26 years earlier. Social media followings were far from being created! God knew my path and knew that I would hit this bump in the road, so specific words were shared in that blessing to help me move through this bump, free of unnecessary detours. Jon shared this information with our church leader and it made an impact on him. Only one week later, he invited me to meet with him and he shared, "I have been given the authority to decide if you are guilty of apostasy or not, and the spirit has impressed upon me greatly that you ARE led by the spirit. You and I might not personally agree on what you share, but God has shared with me that you are truly being led by his guidance. I will never bring this up again unless they ask me to." And he never did.

As I look back, I see that I had the opportunity to learn to trust my truth and share through the gift of my voice, to speak my truth and more powerfully activate my throat chakra, as I was just at the beginning of using it! In that experience, I can also see the old energy of the throat chakra—the expectation that I should only say what is considered acceptable and appropriate for the time. I understand that some of us are called to disrupt the status quo by speaking up, so we can be free of the old Piscean Age energy that no longer serves us. It is my intention to use the new energy of the throat chakra to support me in sharing my truth to help others live theirs.

Remembering Wholeness has sold over 150,000 copies and is a beloved book. I hear on a regular basis from readers how much that book means to them and how powerfully it changed their lives. I would not have been able to share with that many people if I had compromised my voice. I hope to think that my act of staying the course, helped open the energy for others to follow and share their truths, free of opposition or judgment. Energy healing is still odd to some, but I think we can all say that alternative health practices have hit the mainstream in the time in which we live.

I was blessed by God and the new energy of the throat chakra to help me move through an experience that I easily could have created a lot of pain and struggle for me. I could have created a perception that I was a victim of men in authority. But if I had, I would just be repeating my childhood story! By staying true to both my own power and my voice, I could move through the experience of the old energy, without it compromising me. As you tap into the new energy of the throat chakra, you will speak your truth in a manner that dearly blesses your life and the lives of others.

THE NEW ENERGY OF THE THROAT CHAKRA

We live at a remarkable time that can be overwhelming if we don't manage it well with boundaries. I am referring to the remarkable experience of living in the "information age." Our throat chakra energy is being activated, and for many, it feels like overload. Let's look at some examples of how this activated energy shows up in our daily lives. According to an article at Forbes, 3.7 billion people are now internet users. Every second of the day, Google processes over 40,000 searches, which adds up to 3.5 billion searches per day. On average, every minute of the day:

- *Snapchat users share 527,760 photos*
- *More than 120 professionals join LinkedIn*
- *Users watch 4,146,600 YouTube videos*
- *456,000 tweets are sent on Twitter*
- *Instagram users post 46,740 photos* [33]

Wow! I am going to go take a nap! That data is from May 2018, and doesn't even include the Facebook stats! Phew. Our throat chakras are definitely being activated and they are on overload for many!

The following are indicators that the new energy of the 5th chakra is getting activated for you and you are feeling more and more that it's time to speak your truth. How many of these have you experienced?

- You notice when you don't say what you really want to say and it's becoming increasingly uncomfortable for you to do so.
- You are more aware of wanting to voice your opinion, yet you fear or are concerned about retaliation or pushback from others.
- You are tired of thinking you have to say what you think others want you to say, and you just want to speak up for yourself.
- You realize your voice has shut down in your life and are in the process of healing that.

- You admire people who can speak with confidence and share what is correct for them in a civil and respectful way. You desire to be able to do that.
- You have noticed that you get colds, sore throats, coughs more often than should be normal.
- You'd like to be an influence for good to other people and you realize that means that you need better communication skills.
- You want to be able to express how you feel and what you want clearly with confidence.

WHAT DO YOU WANT TO SAY?

What are you doing to use your voice that matters? Or are you just adding noise to the energetic environment in which we live? With so much being said and shared in the world, I have come to really consider whether what I am saying is worth being said.

In our day-to-day lives, we use our voices in different situations, with different circles of people. How confidently do you express your authentic self with certain people? Look at the following list and rate yourself on a scale of 1–5. 1 = I don't express myself authentically with that person. 5 = I express myself confidently with that person or people all the time:

1. Your own self-talk
2. Your significant other
3. Your children
4. Extended family
5. Friends
6. Work associates
7. Professional or public roles
8. Social media spaces

How did you do? I'll share my answers to help you reflect on your own experience, as well as some tips to help you speak more authentically:

Self-talk

I want to be 100% honest with myself, free of delusions and blocks that would keep me stuck, so much that I even include the following in my prayers: "God, thank you for helping me see and be aware of anything that I am not seeing or owning. Help me be free of any delusions and blocks that are keeping me stuck. Thank you for making it very clear to me." I give myself a 5.

If you have a lot of negative self-talk, you may be telling yourself a lot of delusional things. My thoughts are no longer full of shaming or negative self-talk. I have trained my mind to think in the affirmative over the years. It takes practice, but you can do it. Pay attention to the thoughts going through your mind today and change negative self-talk to the positive.

SIGNIFICANT OTHER

For me, this has been a work in progress. My husband, Jon, and I are able to be honest and forthcoming with each other as we have worked on speaking authentically in our marriage. The first 10 years of our marriage were riddled with pain and confusion that had to be sorted from the childhood wounding we both brought to the partnership. Once we got involved in healing our lives, we started to get more honest with ourselves and each other. I give myself a 5.

This can be a challenging space to choose to speak your truth. If you lack confidence or feel you have to accommodate your partner by only talking about what they want to hear, I recommend you work on your 3rd chakra (the power chakra) and also the 4th chakra (the heart chakra). When you speak your truth with confidence and love, it will be heard and will help your partner, whether they outwardly show you that it's helpful or not. Speaking your truth does not mean sharing every little thing. Some things are just not meant to be shared, but are meant to be for your experience.

Children

When it comes to speaking my truth with my children, that does not mean I tell them everything, and they don't tell me everything. It means sharing authentically, and in a way that is appropriate for a parent-child relationship. When my children were small, I invited them to tell me when anything I said caused them to feel fear or shame by using the following statement: "Mom, how you are talking to me right now is scaring me. Please change your tone of voice." Or, "Mom, what you are saying to me right now is making me feel bad. Please don't do that." I didn't have a voice growing up. I was too scared to ever speak up and was a very quiet child. I was taught to "not rock the boat" for my father's sake. We walked on eggshells so he wouldn't get upset out of the blue. Growing up in fear and being taught that anything you said could tip my father into unjustifiable rage set me up to want to find and use my voice to make a difference. I did not want my children to be silenced out of fear. I did not want anything I said to shame them. I heard shaming things from my father through the years, and I wanted better for my children. I gave them words to use as tools to do that. Did they use them? Yes. Did I respond favorably? You bet I did! Accountability is very high on my list and I hold myself to it first.

I do not meddle or share my two cents as a mother and mother-in-law with my adult children. I wait until I am invited. If they seek me out for guidance or feedback, I offer my thoughts, insights, and inspirations with them. Some of my children seek me out for this more than others. That is fine. I am grateful this one has been easy for me. I have a busy life and honestly don't spend time assessing their life situations. I trust that if I am meant to be a support to any of them, the opportunity will present itself. I also feel it is not supportive to turn to them with any relationship challenges I may be working through. They witnessed enough of the challenging relationship my husband and I have recovered from; they really don't need to be involved anymore in that. I give myself a 5.

As you practice speaking more authentically with your children, I caution you to not turn to your children as your support system. They can be your friends and allies, but to seek them out to play a role of a parent or guide for you reverses the energy of your relationship in an unhealthy way. Remember the story of Sam in Part One of the book? His parents put too much pressure on him to carry their emotional energy. That's what I'm talking about! And don't meddle or give feedback unless they ask you. That is not a good use of your throat chakra energy; it will just feel intrusive to your kids.

Extended family

This is still the most challenging space for me to feel I have a voice and use it. I have three siblings with strong personalities and a lot to say. When you grow up in a family where you can't express yourself openly, you tend to want to make up for it in your adult years once you find your voice! Being the only female sibling has been part of the scenario and I am not very close to any of my brothers. I am still quite silent if there is a meeting or gathering of us, which does not happen very often. I notice it and know I am not being myself, but I do feel like it is a conscious choice, rather than one provoked by fear. I give myself a 3.

What roles do you play in your extended family? Do those roles allow you to use your voice authentically? If you do not speak authentically in these situations, pay attention to the emotion feeding that experience. Fear can be a big factor in extended family communication. The sooner you recognize if fear provokes your response, the sooner you can do something about it.

Friends

As a personal choice, I do not have many friends. My time is valuable to me and I believe friendships take time and effort. About the few friends I do have, I would say I am more open with some than others. I am always authentic, yet I am not comfortable sharing all aspects of my life with some friends. I give myself a 4.

Some people feel safer to be more authentic and honest with their friends than they are with their partner. If this describes you, ask yourself why you feel safer to be your true self and say the truth in your friend relationships than your intimate relationship. Once you identify the variable that helps you feel supported, set an intention you are going to create the same relationship climate with your partner, so you feel safe to speak what is true for you.

Work associates

My work associates are employees of the company I own. The most challenging work-employee relationship I had to navigate has been with my CEOs. My son served in the role of CEO for several years and did a fantastic job helping us create a strong online foundation that helped me take my Dressing Your Truth system to the world. By the time he left employment with me, the company had grown to reach women in over 110 countries. Ultimately, he left because we each couldn't be ourselves and lead the company with two visions that were not always the same. He had his vision and voiced it, and I had mine. For a few years leading up to his departure, I held my voice back. He was the child I had the most delicate relationship with, as I didn't know his nature when he was a child and I could easily steamroll him. I made a great effort not to do that in our working relationship, but to a fault. I compromised myself more than was healthy or appropriate for me. I wasn't speaking my truth; I was following his. This came to head for both of us, as we were dealing with issues that would not get resolved by any other means. In a manner, we were forced to deal with the issue. Maybe that prayer I mentioned earlier had something to do with it.

The bottom line was, we both knew that if I followed his vision, I would be compromised—and if he followed my vision, *he* would be compromised. I remember saying to him as we talked about this emotional situation, "I feel like you are building your own company with the company I started." He is a mature and wise young man, and he could see what I meant, and agreed that it had turned into that. I raised my son to be true to himself, and for that I am grateful. He ultimately decided to part business ways with me and is a successful business owner now pursuing his own online marketing ventures.

After he left, I invited my son-in-law to be my CEO. We both have similar natures, so we see eye to eye pretty easily, but we still had to navigate the question of "who is in charge." After our first year of some tough periods to navigate, we finally figured out a solution. Every Monday morning, we meet and the first question he asks me as the visionary of the company is this: "Is there anything the company would want me to know that needs attention?" If there is, I share it. If not, I say no. As an empath, I can communicate with the entity energy of the company and sense what is out of balance. He takes feedback from me and has the ultimate authority to make decisions. I respect his role and I never override him. If I feel differently, we talk about it in a Monday meeting. I've also learned about myself that I can make things matter that don't matter, and I remind myself of that. I do still hesitate at times, but I am aware of when I do that, so I give myself a 4.

What is your work communication like? Do you hold back out of fear of being reprimanded? After you don't say what you want to really say, do you complain to others about it? Have you gotten into trouble by speaking up? What is the environment of your work experience? Are you encouraged to say it how it is? Do you get pushback if you do? Some of your challenges in this space may be old programming you are ready to clear, especially if it keeps showing up. In addition to the chakra-activating session at the end of this chapter, I offer numerous clearing sessions in The Carol Tuttle Healing Center to help you have the experience of speaking your truth.

Professional roles

Are you in a professional or public role that supports you in speaking your truth? I am! With my previous story that I shared in this section, I have been given many opportunities to learn how to do that with confidence. I give myself a 5.

Where can you use your voice in professional spaces? What is calling to be said? If you are holding back because you worry about others' responses, consider the possibility that they are actually waiting for you to be a different voice in that space.

Social media spaces

I only use social media for business purposes, so I do not have a personal experience with it to share. I have noticed that to a large degree, people use social media as a platform to vent! They say what is bothering them so openly, possibly because nobody else seems to be listening in other spaces. I can't really rate myself here, as I don't have personal experience with it.

Social media is a space to share yourself in nearly any way you want these days. How are you using it? Go look at your last few posts. Are they venting? What are you putting your attention on—and asking others to put their attention on?

It is important to speak your truth in all of these communication experiences where communication is part of the experience. I believe it's important that you feel you have a choice, rather than feeling dictated by fear. Does using your throat chakra always include your speaking voice when you speak your truth? Not necessarily.

You may be more comfortable speaking your truth through your singing voice, your musical voice, your written voice, your artistic voice, which take a strong 2nd chakra to support you with. The variable to consider regarding whether you're tapping into the new energy of the throat chakra is to ask yourself: Am I hesitant to speak my truth here due to fear? Or am I choosing not to speak my truth here as I feel that is what is most supportive to me and the situation at hand?

THE NEW EXPERIENCE OF "BEING INFLUENCED"

Only in the last 50 years has the role of influencing humanity shifted away from primarily religious and government leaders to potentially anybody with access to the internet, using a phone or laptop.

YouTube became the first online video platform to launch the new wave of the common person playing the role of an influencer, as the focal point of most of the early videos was people speaking and teaching. The influencers who grew out of that platform didn't have to have any particular role or formal position that gave them authority to influence other people. If you're on YouTube, everyday people get to decide if you are worthy of influencing them!

After YouTube, numerous other social media platforms made it possible for us to share our thoughts and upload videos instantly. Facebook, Instagram, Twitter, and Snapchat gave people a platform to play out their role of influencer. Television media experienced a major shift from the monolithic networks to a variety of online streaming platforms. Hollywood celebrities still seem to be popular with younger audiences, but as we mature, we drop those voices out of our lives to seek for more self-understanding and wisdom.

Take an inventory of the people who are influencing your life. Which people do you allow the role of influencer in your life? I assume I am one of them if you are reading this right now! Because there are so many options of people to follow and be influenced by, what is your criteria that influencer needs to meet for you? Have you thought about that? Have you spoken to your children about creating a criteria for themselves so they can filter out noise and seek out value? There is more information coming at us than ever in the history of the world. The throat chakra is wide open and very active. Make sure you only allow what adds value to your life and to your world.

THINKING BEFORE YOU SPEAK

You may think I am referring to the old adage, "think before you speak"—meaning, don't say anything you would regret, or that might be hurtful to another, or that might embarrass you if you don't know enough about what you are saying. That is all good advice, but I am using this in a different connotation. I am referring to the habit of having to think over what you are going to say before you say it. Do you ever do this? How often?

If you overthink your words, you don't speak what you want imme-diately. You process it first by considering how others will respond to you, what they might say back, what they will think of you, and if they will agree with you. After you speak, do you assess and go over what you just said, evaluating and judging it, regretting it, or feeling stupid for it?

This habit is a sign that your throat chakra is weak. When your throat chakra is clear and open, you have an ability to discern very quickly when to speak, when to keep quiet, which words to use, and how to say it with confidence. You feel comfortable about what you shared and have no need to review it. This saves you a lot of energy as the old habit is exhausting. To shift this habit, start noticing when you do it, and think this affirmation to start opening your throat chakra: "I am confident in what I have to say. Others hear me and support me."

LISTENING IS SPEAKING—FOR THE EXTROVERTS

Anyone can activate their throat chakra, but different people will use that energy in different ways. Some people are more extroverted in the use of their energy, moving outward first. Others move inward first, which makes them more introverted. This affects how they experience their throat chakra energy.

I would consider myself a throat chakra extrovert. That does not mean I am a highly social person. It means that I speak up in situa-tions more often than not. I am probably the most quiet in larger social gatherings, but most other places, I can use my voice with confidence. Because of my extrovert throat chakra energy, I can have a tendency to talk more than listen.

In fact, I have had a tendency to talk too much when I am with oth-ers. Part of this is a result of growing up in a household of not being able to talk openly. Another part is just not being mindful in the moment.

I have worked on this for many years, and still have opportunities to tell myself, things like, "You don't need to say that." "What others have shared is enough." You just interrupted that person, stop talking, apologize, and ask them to finish." "Will you add any value to the conversation by sharing that?" "Why don't you practice listening right now, and really hear what they are saying."

Do you talk more than others when you are in a group? Do you interrupt or finish people's sentences? Do you think people take too long to say what they are saying so you try and hurry them up? You may be a throat chakra extrovert.

Throat chakra extroverts get a bad rap when they don't manage their energy around others. Others feel the energy pouring out of their mouths and filling up the space, not leaving room for others to share and add to the experience. If you have a tendency to dominate conversations with an overactive throat chakra, notice and practice creating a stronger habit to listen. Let others speak what wants to be spoken by choosing to listen and creating a space for it.

SPEAKING IS LISTENING—FOR THE INTROVERTS

A throat chakra introvert is someone who tends to speak less and keep things to themselves. They have a tendency to listen more than they talk. When this tendency is out of balance, nobody gets to hear what they have to say. If this describes you, ask yourself: Why do I do that? Is it too hard to get a word in edgewise? Do you think you don't have something valuable to share? Do you think other people aren't worthy to hear it? Or that it won't matter anyway, so why bother? What is the reason?

As our throat chakra energy gets healthy and balanced, everyone gets to have a say and what they say matters. You have wisdom and value to share that others would benefit from listening to. You may have heard the phrase, "giving and receiving are the same." When you give, you receive something from it. What goes out, returns to you multiplied. You reap what you sow. And in the immediate act of giving, you receive the blessing of feeling grateful to have had the chance to give and make a difference.

Consider the possibility that speaking and listening are the same. When you speak, you hear yourself and receive the value of what you have to share. When you listen, you receive the value of what others share and when you agree, it's as if you spoke it. Many people have shared thanks with me over the years for what I said, or what I wrote. They say, "You spoke what I was feeling," or, "You gave me the words to make sense of what is happening in my life." I spoke, they listened, and now they can speak their own truth with more clarity.

If any excuses are keeping you from speaking up, set an intention that it will be increasingly uncomfortable for you to stay silent when you are meant to speak. Others want to listen to you, as what you have to say matters and can make the difference of someone also speaking what is true for them.

As a throat chakra introvert, appreciate and use your gift of listening when it is in balance. You don't *need* to speak up unless you're keeping quiet for reasons of fear, shame, or frustration. Your gift of listening is also powerful.

IS YOUR EMOTIONAL ENERGY MESSING WITH YOUR THROAT CHAKRA?

I love the guidance often attributed to the poet-philosopher Rumi called, "The Three Gates of Speech."

Before you speak, let your words pass through three gates:
At the first gate, ask yourself "Is it true?"

At the second gate ask, "Is it necessary?"
At the third gate ask, "Is it kind?"

When we are flooded with emotion, we tend to not have the discipline to ask ourselves these questions and we either fall prey to saying things we regret or not saying anything at all. We verbally overreact or we shut down. When you get emotionally triggered, which direction do your emotions take you? If you fall into the overreacting category, your emotional energy puts your throat chakra into overdrive. If you fall into the shutting-down category, your emotional energy blocks your throat chakra.

The best thing to do when you are emotionally flooded is to not say anything, excuse yourself, and go take care of your emotions. In the time in which we live, people can sense and feel if you are processing emotion. It's very hard to hide, as energy is powerfully expressing itself these days. If you are emotionally triggered when dealing with a family member, politely let them know you're too emotional to have a reasonable conversation and you'd like to wait until you can. If you are in a group or work situation, just stay quiet until the emotions pass. If they do not pass quickly, acknowledge how you are feeling and commit to doing some healing work around what the emotions are telling you.

I fall into the overreacting category and my husband falls in to the shutting-down category. When we were emotionally triggered, neither one of us could communicate effectively. Because I was the louder one and he appeared to stay composed (even though he was just blocked), I would get the blame. Over the years, as we became responsible for our emotional energy and set boundaries with each other by using our voices, sharing either, "Excuse me, I need to take care of my emotions before I can talk about this," or, "It appears you are too emotional to have a reasonable conversation about this let me know when you are more clear because I want to work this out." Once the emotions settled down, we used effective communication tools to come to mutually agreeable decisions and resolve.

USE YOUR WORDS

"Use your words" has become a popular phrase used by parents with small children who whine and fuss to ask for what they want. It's a good reminder for all of us. If you "beat around the bush" and hope people pick up on clues about what you want, you are not using your words. If a situation in your life is asking you to use your words to set appropriate boundaries and you do not use them, the situation will continue to play out and you'll continue to feel powerless. If you have a need or a want in your relationship and you hope your partner is in tune enough, because if they loved you they would just know, you'll be disappointed when it doesn't happen. Use your words!

What is showing up in your life right now that is asking for you to "use your words"? Why do you hesitate? Know that this situation will keep showing up until you learn to speak your truth and use your words, as that is the new energy lesson of the throat chakra.

Exercises to Strengthen the New Energy of the Throat Chakra

Use any and all of the following exercises to help you ground the new energy of the throat chakra into your personal energy system. You can use them as frequently as you find supportive.

Reading Out Loud

If you have a habit of not speaking up and staying quiet, reading out loud is a simple way to help you start hearing yourself speak out loud. It will help you practice using your voice with different words and phrases. Speaking out loud activates the new energy of the throat chakra, as you don't have to think about what you are saying—you just say what you are reading.

Singing in a Choir

Join a choir to help open your voice. As you sing with others, you will receive other benefits as well, such as a common interest that you can talk to each other about, a sense of belonging, and a great way to share your voice with others.

Taking Voice Lessons

Taking voice lessons will activate the new energy of the throat chakra by exercising your vocal cords and teaching you how to breathe deeply to sing properly. You also have a chance to overcome a fear of expressing yourself with your voice in a new form. Vocal exercises open the energy to support you in speaking your truth in all areas of your life.

Practicing Listening

If you have an extrovert throat chakra, practice listening more and speaking less. Before you speak, let your words pass through Rumi's Three Gates of true, necessary, and kind.

Watching the Movie The King's Speech

Who would guess that a movie could help you activate your throat chakra? Britain's Prince Albert must ascend the throne as King George VI, but he has a speech impediment. A speech therapist named Lionel is hired to help him overcome his stammer. The speech therapist uses unconventional methods to teach the monarch how to speak with confidence. You can do the exercises right along with the King while watching the movie! And watching the extraordinary friendship that develops as Lionel helps the King believe in himself will not only open your throat chakra, but your heart chakra, too.

Writing a Letter to Your Inner Child and Inviting Them to Reply

One reason your throat chakra is blocked is because you didn't get to develop it in your childhood. Inviting your inner child to express what was never expressed during childhood will open your throat chakra. If you grew up in the energy of "children should be seen and not heard," then this exercise will be important for you to give voice to that part of you. Just follow these steps:

1. Using your dominant hand, write the following: "Dear Little Self, How are you? Thank you for finishing the following sentence to let me know how you are feeling."
2. Using your non-dominant hand, to mimic a child's handwriting, finish this sentence at least 10 times, "Dear Big Self, I am feeling…"
3. Continue this process with both hands, using open-ended sentences to prompt the part of you that was told they had to stay quiet. This exercise will give a voice to a part of you that deserves to be heard.

Walking Your Talk

The throat chakra wants to partner with the root chakra so we can experience the feeling that, "I walk my talk." This exercise will connect the higher frequency of the throat chakra to raise the frequency of the root chakra, creating an electrical current between these two energy centers.

1. Sit in a comfortable position with your arms and legs uncrossed. Take three deep, relaxing, cleansing breaths.
2. Place one hand on the root chakra at your pelvic bone, and the other on the throat chakra at the center of your neck.
3. To help connect these energies and help them to work together, rotate your hands between each chakra, switching your hands from the root to the throat at the same time, doing this seven times.
4. Tell the root chakra that it is now being coached by the throat chakra. The throat chakra is going to teach the root chakra how to walk your talk!

Finding Your Voice With Essential Oils

Massage a few drops of essential oils on the location of the 5th chakra on the throat. Carol Tuttle Healing Oils are custom blends that support you with specific healing goals. These oil blends can be used to activate and strengthen the throat chakra in the following ways:

- **I am connected:** This oil will assist you in staying present with your own thoughts and feelings, so you can express what is correct and timely for you to express.
- **I am confident:** This oil will assist you in having confidence in your thoughts and ideas, and the confidence to express them clearly and thoughtfully.

What key thing did you learn from this section?

Use this space to make notes. Write down questions and insights you had while reading this section.

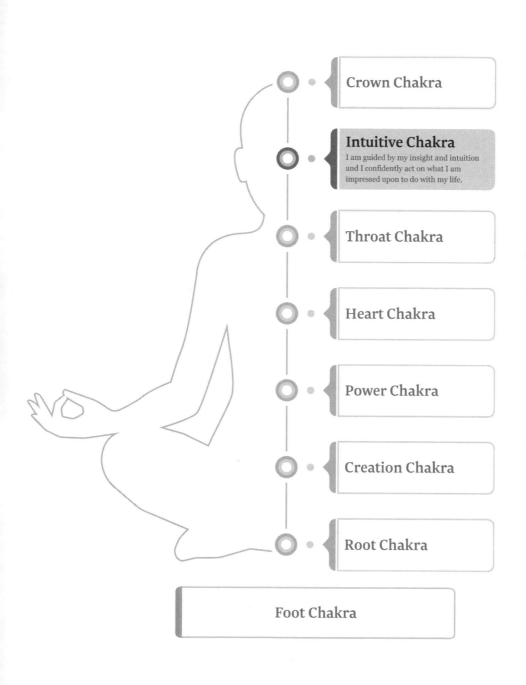

Crown Chakra

Intuitive Chakra
I am guided by my insight and intuition
and I confidently act on what I am
impressed upon to do with my life.

Throat Chakra

Heart Chakra

Power Chakra

Creation Chakra

Root Chakra

Foot Chakra

Step 6: Activating Your Intuition

• • • • • • •

6th Chakra—The Intuitive Chakra

Location:	The middle of the forehead and upper backside of the head.
Yin/Yang Flow:	Yin energy, with the energy moving inward as we seek insight and strengthen our inner knowing.
Universal Color:	Indigo
Associated Organs and Body Parts:	Head, pituitary gland, eyes, lower part of the brain. Imbalance in this chakra can be connected to headaches, dizziness, blindness, and mental fog.
Function:	Energetically connecting us to our intuition and psychic gifts, self-reflection, visualization, discernment and trust in our own knowing.
Old Energy:	Using the logical mind to observe the outer world so we can make survival decision and prevent "bad" things from happening in our life.
New Energy:	I am turning within to follow my own insight and intuition to guide my decisions in doing what is correct for me in living my truth.
If Closed:	You feel disconnected from your intuition, or feel like you don't have any. You feel lost when it comes to your own spiritual purpose and path in life. You turn to others for validation and permission to move forward in your life. You get headaches and often feel tension in your brow area.
If Open:	Your intuition is your constant guide that you trust. You have a strong sense of your own inner truth and you listen to and follow it as it guides you on your life path. You act in confidence based on your intuition.
Affirmation:	I am guided by my insight and intuition and I confidently act on what I am impressed upon to do with my life.
Carol Tuttle Healing Oil Blends:	I am present I am purpose

The sixth step in awakening brings us into the intuitive chakra energy. The intuitive chakra is nicknamed the "third eye" in reference to insight. This chakra is all about inner vision and inner understanding of our unseen, inner world.

The inner world is comprised of our thoughts, feelings, visions, impressions, promptings, knowings, spiritual hits, and psychic abilities. In the year 2000, I wrote about these psychic abilities in my book *Remembering Wholeness* in the section titled, "Everyone is Psychic." At that time, few people talked openly about these things. That has changed as a result of the intuitive chakra energy turning on more and more of our psychic abilities. In *Remembering Wholeness,* I teach the following about our psychic gifts and talents:

> *"Webster's Dictionary defines the word psychic as someone who communicates with spirit. The American Heritage Dictionary defines it as extraordinary, extrasensory and nonphysical, mental processes.*
>
> *According to the above definitions, everyone is psychic because everyone has spiritual gifts and capacities he or she is meant to be using more intimately to guide and direct his or her life. We have become conditioned to using our physical senses and logical thinking minds as the compass of our lives. By fine-tuning our spiritual senses, we will be able to choose more effortlessly, with fewer and fewer detours, the direction our lives could be taking.*
>
> *Spiritual gifts include intuition, discernment, precognition, spiritual empathy, visionary, working of miracles, powers of healing and powers to be healed."* [34]

It has been uncomfortable for most people to share the inner gifts and qualities that are very much a part of them with others. We tend to believe if we can't see it, we can't trust it. Yet, many people's inner world is as active and real as their outer world, due to their powerful intuitive chakra that has been active since birth. More and more, children are coming into the world with the new energy of the intuitive chakra intact. It's wise to learn about the old energy of the third chakra and how the new energy is changing that experience for all of us.

THE OLD ENERGY OF THE INTUITIVE CHAKRA

The old energy that humanity was locked into for centuries was the practice of looking outside the self for answers and needing explanation or visible claims of what is accurate and viable.

Are you still living in the old energy of looking to others to know what is correct for you? Do you look to others for validation and permission? Are you a skeptic unless something has a logical explanation or physical proof? With the way our intuition works, it's common for us to get a hit—an insight, a strong internal impression of what is correct for us—that comes through a feeling, a sense, a body sensation, or an image in our minds and then have the logical mind start to question and examine the awareness that is starting to form. When the logical mind gets involved in the intuitive mind's process of guiding us, the logical mind usually wins out. It's like the logical mind is the bigger, stronger adult and the intuitive mind is the vulnerable, small child. Looking outside of ourselves for answers is the old energy that will actually keep us stuck and spiraling in uncertainty. Due to beliefs that have been held by generations in your own family system, you could easily be sabotaging your intuition from growing.

The intellectual mind is a grand tool. We need it to navigate our outer world happenings, but it is not a very good guidance system in today's world, where we have more energetic freedom than we have ever had. There are no longer cultural constructs dictating our choices. The walls have been removed and it's up to us to determine what is correct and not correct for us. It is up to us to find our own path. I have found that people who carry these two limiting beliefs (looking outside themselves and looking for proof) will often keep their intuitive mind stifled and blocked. By identifying which limiting beliefs you carry, you can open up and activate this chakra.

LIMITING BELIEF: "IT WORKS FOR EVERYONE ELSE BUT ME!"

This common belief is formed in childhood and it can stunt our access to intuition. As children, many of us experienced the repeated cycle of hoping for something to happen and then when it didn't, we were hugely disappointed. In order to prevent more episodes of ongoing disappointment when we were children, we adopted the belief of, "It won't happen for me." This belief kept us from getting our hopes up, in an effort to avoid disappointment yet once again.

This limiting belief will block our intuitive mind from speaking to us. Intuition feeds off of hope and when we have shut down our hope, we also shut down our intuition. If that feels true for you on any level, you will benefit from this insight shared by a member of The Carol Tuttle Healing Center:

> "I recently read some posts from other members about how some haven't felt any different after doing several clearings and some may have even gone through a whole healing plan without noticing a shift. I want to share my experience. I felt like this, too. I read

everyone's a-ha moments or feeling a shift. I hadn't experienced these things. I kept wondering what was I doing wrong? And thought, 'Why do things always work for everyone else but not for me?' Bam. There was my a-ha moment, I asked what to do when I carried the belief of, 'It works for everyone else but not for me.' It was suggested I do the clearing walk [a process taught in the Healing Center], and I did it. I said something to the effect of, 'It works for everyone including me.' Here are some of the resistance statements that came up: You don't deserve it. You're not special enough. Don't get your hopes up, you'll only be disappointed, You won't get as much attention if you heal. If you haven't felt a shift or had a-ha moments, keep at it. Your intuition and healing experience will open and activate. It has to—it happened for me!"

Helping my clients clear this limiting belief was something I did in my private practice. If a client came in after three or four weeks of doing sessions with me and shared, "It's not working," I knew that they had this belief of, "It works for everyone else but not for me." You may still hold that belief because it was probably true in your childhood. That's fair, but a more accurate way to describe those unmet hopes from your childhood is to say, "My parents did not follow through on what they said they would do," or, "I was led to believe something that wasn't true and I blamed myself," or, "I wasn't taught how to deal with disappointment as an experience of life; I just believed it didn't work out for me because I thought I wasn't worth it." Those are the more accurate statements of what you experienced as a child. And you are not a child anymore. You can decide that it *can* work out and will work out for you! Believing in possibilities and generating hope again sends a powerful life force energy into your 6th chakra to turn on your intuition.

You need hope as a foundation to your intuition as intuition is a function of believing in something that has not happened, and sometimes does not make sense logically or have any physical evidence to support it. Which leads me to the next limiting belief that can sabotage your intuitive mind.

LIMITING BELIEF: "IF YOU CAN'T PROVE IT, DON'T TRUST IT."

A skeptic is someone who is inclined to question or doubt ideas, phenomena, or popular opinion. They prefer facts and evidence to support what they believe. I agree that we shouldn't just go along with everything that is or has become popular in today's world. There is so much out there, that we all benefit from a dose of skepticism. But if you turn your skepticism toward your own inner workings of intuition, you require your intellectual mind to depend on itself at a time when that is also tricky. What if you taught your intellectual mind and intuitive mind to work as partners, so it's not an all-or-nothing or either/or experience? Which decisions in your life are best based on logical information guiding you? Which decisions are best made from your intuition guiding you? A partnership between the thinking mind and the intuitive mind is a powerful set-up to navigate the modern world of "anything goes."

When it comes to dealing with other people who are skeptics, let people be on their own journey. It's very deflating to try and convince someone who has a firm belief that if you can't prove it, don't trust it. Your inner world is your sacred space and meant for you first. Whether you share it with others or not, please use discretion. Intuition is a feeling and a mental clarity that cannot be rationalized. Be wise in who you choose to share your inspirations with. A skeptic's skepticism may add to any of your own doubts.

THE NEW ENERGY OF THE INTUITIVE CHAKRA

The new energy of the intuitive chakra is turning our attention inward to explore and open our inner world of self. It is teaching the intellectual mind to partner with the intuitive mind to not depend on intellect alone, but to trust the inner knowing of self that will actually be a great coach and guide to the intellectual mind.

We can see evidence of the intuitive chakra's new energetic influence in the increased interest in and practice of meditation. The most popular online app to help people with meditation practices is called Headspace, with over 30 million users worldwide.[35] What used to be seen as an experience only monks practiced has become an accepted, modern-day self-help tool.

The following are indicators that the new energy of the 6th chakra is getting activated for you and you are feeling drawn to turn within to follow your intuition. How many of these have you experienced?

- You can't seem to find clarity on some things in your life, no matter how much you go over and over it in your thoughts.
- You experience a sense of knowing what is next and what is correct for you, but you are hesitant to follow through on it in case you are wrong.
- You have shared some of your more spiritual experiences with skeptical people and experienced some sort of backlash.
- You feel drawn to meditation and spending time quieting your mind and turning within.
- You are feeling nudges to make some changes and you want to know for sure what is correct for you.

- You know what other people are feeling. You often feel what they are feeling and it's often not pleasant and you pay a price for it.
- You are wanting to sleep longer than usual. You often have more vivid dreams.

This spiritual awakening is happening to everyone. Our empath abilities are being heightened, which means you know or feel what other people are feeling and oftentimes what they are thinking! The challenge for most people is, they don't know what to do with this ability, and have not developed energetic boundaries yet, so they end up taking the energy into their own system. Very few people openly talked about these experiences of the unseen world, but that has shifted and come into the forefront in the last decade.

Have you had an inner spiritual awakening of some sort? How would you describe it? Do you feel like your psychic gifts have been turned on? By trusting your intuition, you are brought the physical evidence of making the right choice soon after the decision. As you continue this cycle of allowing the inspirations to come, acting on them, followed by positive results, your intuition will continue to grow and become very strong and natural. It will become the primary way of knowing which choices to make and what direction to move in life.

Intuition and all other spiritual gifts are powers given to us by God that are to be trusted and acted upon. By not using them, they become dormant and absent to us. Ask God to help you know what your spiritual gifts are and how to implement them into your daily experience. All spiritual gifts are available to everyone. If there are any gifts you would like to have, just ask that they be given to you. Let go of the limiting beliefs that keep you from experiencing these gifts.

10 WAYS TO KNOW YOUR INTUITION IS TRYING TO TELL YOU SOMETHING

When you are dealing with an issue or a life-changing decision, you probably do one of two things: ask others for their advice on the matter or listen to your own intuition. I have learned that it is best to choose the second option first! Sometimes the guidance you or I receive from others might not be the right advice at all. In fact, it may be better for us to just listen to our intuition instead. But if you don't know how to listen to it, that can be a challenge. Learning to listen to your intuition supports your intuition in getting stronger, and as it gets stronger, it is easier to listen to. So how do you listen to your intuition or even identify what it is?

Licensed clinical psychologist Sarah Schewitz states:

"Intuition is that sneaking suspicion that you feel when something is not right but you can't put your finger on why. Intuition can be a powerful guiding force and is more developed for some than others. Some people feel a strong urge or sense in their core when something is wrong while others, with a less-developed intuition, might feel a small inkling that they aren't really sure how to interpret it. Some people are born with a strong intuition and know how to listen to it from an early age, whereas others develop their intuition or tune into it as they grow a stronger sense of self-confidence. The more that you love and trust yourself, the more in touch you become with your intuition."[36]

The first thing to notice when making a decision is if your decision is provoked by fear, guilt, shame, or an effort to prevent something you don't want. Your intuition does not talk to you in terms of, "I'm not good enough," "I'm not worthy," "I'm not ready or prepared," "What if I fail?" "What if I succeed?" or "What if I humiliate myself?" Any decision made out of fear or doubt is usually never a good decision. Intuition speaks to us in the positive, even if it's a warning of some kind. The language of our intuition is a language of love, not self-doubt. When you listen to your intuition you should feel empowered, rather than scared or worried.

Here are 10 ways to know if your intuition is trying to tell you something, plus tips to help you follow it. Your intuition is trying to tell you something if:

You feel a peaceful feeling somewhere in your body.

For most people, the place in the body where they feel peace is in the chest or stomach. I have also had clients share they experience this feeling in their head—a peace of mind. When something is "off" in our lives, it's common to feel a tightness in our stomach, chest, or head, so knowing the difference in your body's response is a good way to know your intuition is talking to you.

You have a sense of confidence even when the decision seems irrational.

Your intuition may be telling you to move forward with something new, such as a move or a new career venture. You might have dismissed this as a daydream. You can know your intuition is getting your attention if it becomes increasingly more uncomfortable to keep doing what you are doing. What have you been dreaming about? Don't wait until you are free of uncertainty to follow your intuition. Your logical mind thinks in rational terms, which is different from how your intuitive mind works. Your intuitive mind can be confident, even when your rational mind does not have all the details.

You are getting insights in your dreams.

Intuition can come in many forms. Dreams are a way that we received messages that come from beyond us. Because intuition often does not have a specific time stamp, sometimes we can intuitively pick up things about our past, present, and future. Pay attention to your dreams for a week. Write them down when you wake up and see what emerges.

The same opportunity keeps knocking on your door.

I knew that my intuition was trying to talk to me in the early 1990s because the same information showed up in my life three times in a matter of a week. I was looking for ways to heal my life and the same answer kept showing up. I paid attention and the opportunity presented itself to study Reiki and then Rapid Eye Technology. My rational mind thought it was weird, but the healing results I experienced very quickly was my soul's way of saying to me, "This works. It's not a well-traveled path yet, but you are someone who will help make that path more available to other people." What's been trying to get your attention? Look into it.

You experience moments of clarity.

Have you ever had those "a-ha!" moments when you were in the shower or driving your car or doing something else mundane? Something suddenly comes to you in those moments. That's an example of your intuition trying to talk to you. Your intuition talks to you when you are less busy, when you sleep, when are you not trying to push for it, when you take your mind off what you are seeking. If you want to tap into your intuition, what mindless task can you do that will give your intuition space to show up?

Your thoughts are getting clearer and clearer on what is the correct course of action for you.

Your intuition is there to guide you in the right direction, but sometimes you miss the signs or choose to ignore them. It usually just gets stronger if it's something your soul really wants you to pay attention to. If you get intuitive hits about something, and you dismiss them, they will keep showing up in different ways to get your attention.

You feel uncomfortable or uneasy about certain situations.

When you learn to listen to your intuition, you normally feel calm and clear. If you choose to ignore it, you may notice a wave of uneasiness come over you. For instance, I have listened to my intuition for many years now and have fine-tuned communication with my intuitive mind. When I ignore it or go against it, I feel very uneasy and uncomfortable, as if I am forcing something that is not supposed to happen or I am not choosing to do something I am meant to. Your intuition is trying to tell you something when you feel uneasy. Ask to know more clearly what it is trying to help you see.

You may become ill or have physical symptoms.

When you don't listen to your intuition, you may actually cause more stress in your life. Physical signs like having anxiety or being sick may slowly creep into your life because your intuition is trying to tell you that you need a change. When you ignore your intuition in its early stages of trying to get your attention and you don't honor it, it can turn into physical disease or discomfort. Your intuition calls on your body to help you get the message. Our bodies are trying to tell us that we need to make some changes in our life to free up the anxiety and tension it has taken on for us. When you do not live true to yourself, you pay a high price that you no longer need to pay if you will follow the path of what is correct for you.

You feel inspired and motivated.

You know your intuition is speaking to you when you feel inspired and moved. This can happen in a variety of situations, or while you're hearing others' words of wisdom—anything that touches you and sparks your thoughts and insight to follow the path you're meant to be on. Your intuition might manifest as a feeling of happiness or excitement or a desire or impulse to do something creative or beneficial for either yourself or others.

The feeling won't go away!

There's a reason why particular thoughts keep on popping up in your head. Your intuition is trying to speak to you. Be more receptive to these subtle nuances so you can allow your life to flow much more easily. The best way to determine if it is your intuition telling you something is that you will have the sense that it "won't go away." In other words, that sensation of knowing you should or should not do something simply keeps showing up.

Learning how to listen to your intuition takes time. Your ego might try to interfere, but if you practice, you'll eventually know the difference between the two. The more you listen, the happier and secure you will feel about the choices you make.

HOW TO STOP TAKING ON OTHER PEOPLE'S ENERGY AS AN EMPATH

Have you ever had the experience of feeling pretty good, pretty happy, but then you spend time with people who are feeling down, and all of a sudden you start feeling down? Why does that happen? Consider the possibility that you're taking on their emotional energy. As a result of our intuitive chakras being activated into new energy, numerous people are having the experience of being an empath. An empath is someone who can sense and know what others are feeling and even thinking.

So, what does it mean to take on other people's energy? When you are with other people, do you notice what they are feeling, even to the point where you start feeling it too? We offer an energetic vibration to the world that is palpable. You can feel it. Those of us who are empathic are very aware of other people's emotional states and we feel them. My empathic skills have increased to the point that I often can sense what others are thinking in connection with their feelings.

Here's my theory: Some of us grow up in family systems where we didn't talk about what was really going on. Dysfunction played out that nobody put words to. In families like this, there are a lot of feelings that go unexpressed verbally. Most of it was negative. In my case, I had to be aware of anger from my father during my childhood. As a small child, I had to learn to read the energy of the room. I had to make decisions based on what I was reading and sensing. I was constantly assessing: What's going on here? What do I need to be aware of? What do I need to try and prevent? What do I need to steer clear of? How do I navigate this situation so I don't get anybody mad?

How much of that experience feels familiar to you? If you grew up constantly assessing and reading the situation of your family, you may have developed empathic gifts that you wouldn't have otherwise.

Our decisions in our childhood are based on intuiting our space, reading it, and then having to come up with some sort of objective insight as a child. Whatever we encounter as a child is all we know and we think it is normal.

If you consider yourself an empath (or think you might be one), childhood was most likely your first experience at being one. Consider the possibility that you were blessed with this psychic skill when you were young, as you needed it to navigate your childhood. You can discern things. Trust your intuitive awareness of things that are in the energetic realm.

An emotion is a part of the energetic realm. It's a vibration offering that other people can sense or read off of us. Our brain is involved in our emotional response mechanism, but once it's offered, we have a sensory mechanism that's more intuitive and more based on energy that we're able to read. At times, your personal energy system actually becomes congruent and aligned with the person who is running that negative energy and you find yourself vibrating the negative junk right along with the person who is the original author of it!

Wouldn't it be great if you could change that experience to, "I only take on people's joy. I only take on people's enthusiasm." It tends to work the other way around, that you take on the lower vibration, what we classify as a negative emotion. If that sounds like you, you probably did that as a child, as well, as an unspoken, unidentified, subconscious role you played. You could sense that no one was taking accountability for this stuff. And someone has to take accountability. I became the intersection for all of that stuff in my family. Once I became aware in my adult life, I could see how vulnerable I was. I could go into the grocery store feeling great, pass enough people in the aisle who were feeling crummy, and I'd leaving feeling crummy.

Once I understood that I was taking on others' energy, I needed to notice, where does this happen to me? I had to stay aware of where that happened, and who it happened around. It's time for you to be an observer of where you are and who you're with when you take on others' energy.

HOW TO TAKE CARE OF YOUR ENERGY SYSTEM

I was at lunch with a group of women recently, and the woman I sat next to had an interaction that felt awkward for her. Everyone in the group was very polite about it. Based on the response of the women at the luncheon, there was nothing she should have felt ashamed of for any reason, but she had a response of feeling embarrassed. I noticed her emoting that. I was very aware of it, as I was sitting right next to her.

Now in the past, I would have felt that embarrassment with her. I would have joined in emotionally and energetically. Spatially, I was so close that it would have been difficult for me to separate myself. And I would have been right there. When we take on others' energy, we tend to be motivated to try to help them feel better, so that we don't have to feel it, too. Consider the possibility that your efforts to help other people are motivated by your desire to not feel what they're feeling. You want others to feel better so you can stop feeling it. The good news is, you can feel better, even if others don't. Here are two steps to separate your energy so that you can be there for other people, without taking on their energy.

Step 1: Separate Your Energy From Others

In the lunch example, I'd come far enough in my progression that I was able to think this thought: "That is hers." I actually thought that: "That is hers. That is her energy. This is mine. This is my energy. That is her experiencing emotion, and she's going to be fine. Her energy system knows how to work this out." I obviously wasn't doing this visually or out loud. It was in my head. You can do this yourself. You can support the other person by thinking, "You've got this. I'm sending you love and angels and support. Your system's going to work through this uncomfortable feeling, and you're going to be fine. I do not need to join you." Remember that the first step is making a distinction. "That is theirs, that is theirs, this is mine." That's the first step, that distinction. That is theirs, this is mine. You need to create a clear boundary between your energy and the other person's. It may take you a few times to do this so that you're not just melded into it without being able to stay distinctly separate.

Step 2: Just Observe It

Now, my second step in staying in my own energy, was to just observe it. You can be an observer of others having emotional experiences. Just be aware. Your observation can offer support. Picture sending the person the energy of love or inviting angels. Picture them working things out. You want them to. You want people to own their energy, because if you're taking on their energy, they won't get the lesson from their experience.

I have also included another powerful exercise at the end of this section to help you prevent from taking on other people's energy. As you learn to be aware of how other people are feeling without taking on their energy, you can be an energetic influence for good as you hold a higher vibration for them to match rather than you matching their negative one.

MY BIG INTUITIVE WAKE-UP CALL

In 2007, I had what could be called a "spiritual awakening" that powerfully activated my intuitive chakra. I woke up one morning and I knew that my inner world was different. I told my husband, "It's as if all the walls have been removed." I had no judgments, no have-to's, no shoulds or stories to live by—just open space and love. It felt humbling and a bit frightening. I no longer held beliefs that I had to do certain things or achieve certain things from a place of *should* or *have-to*. My motives no longer came from a place of ego and position and I found myself standing in the light within my own inner world only being motivated by goodwill and desire to make a difference. It was as though my inner world had been blown up and none of what I previously held as important really mattered anymore.

For several months, it was challenging to feel motivated to do much. I realized how much my previous inner beliefs had driven me to do things so I didn't feel guilty, or achieve things that made me feel better about myself. I had worked for years to let go of my ego and need to excel, and I thought I had done a pretty good job—until it wasn't there anymore. All I wanted to do was sit and feel the peace and quiet I now had access to inside of me. Fortunately, my practical nature helped me know that doing nothing ultimately wasn't useful to me. But I didn't know how to motivate myself from a different place.

I asked God in prayer, "What am I supposed to do now? I don't feel like I have to do anything! Do I just stop because most of it doesn't matter?" My answer was, "Carol, it does matter but for different reasons than you thought. You are still a part of humanity; use your part to make a difference." I still had a life to do something with. I just had to learn to find a different motivation.

Two years after this inner shift occurred, I chose to go to southern India for a 21-day silent retreat (that means I literally did not talk to anyone for 21 days). I went to learn how to navigate my outer world with such a vastly different set-up in my inner world. I began to learn that my inner world was the best guidance system to choose how to live my life and what to spend my time and energy on. So, I started to ask the question, "Is it correct for me to do this?" Over the last 12 years, I have developed a strong sense of knowing what is correct and what is not correct for me. All I have to do is ask the question and I get a *yes* or *no* immediately. I am highly motivated to do what is correct and it is easy for me to say no to what is not correct. In the past 12 years, I have practiced following my inner guidance and inner vision to motivate me to do what I do. Life has become so much simpler, as I no longer have to entertain what is not correct for me, so I can use my energy for what is correct. I have a peaceful inner world that is very quiet and calm. This shift has allowed me to now live in the present, I no longer have thoughts about the past or future. All there is, is now. I have learned to take inspired action as when I do what is correct, the energy is there to support me in moving forward effortlessly.

Writing this book is a perfect example of how to do what I do with effortless execution. Here's how it played out: I started to feel stirrings that I was meant to write a book about my experience with the chakras in the current time of our lives. The idea wouldn't leave me alone! So I asked the question, "Is it correct to start the chakra book?" The answer was *yes*. That answer came in November 2018. When I write books, the words just come through me. I don't have to think about what I am going to say. I just start to write and it comes. I tried to set aside time for that sort of writing experience every day between November and January, but it wasn't happening. I found it challenging to get in the zone I need in order for the words to come. Yet it was on my mind every day. Many months prior to knowing I would write this book, I had scheduled a five-week trip to our home in Hawaii, for all of February and the first week of March. As that trip drew closer, I had the impression that I was to set apart time while in Hawaii to write. So I asked the question, "Is it correct to write most of the book while I am in Hawaii?" Yes! I even received the intuitive hit that I could get 78% of it written. End of story: I wrote even more than 78% of the book while I was there. It was effortless. I felt like writing every day, the words just came through me and I finished most of the book in just 5½ weeks.

When you follow your inner guidance and do what is correct, the energy lines up so that what you are choosing into feels effortless and magical. You wonder how you could achieve what you achieved. I felt that way about this book that I basically wrote in 5½ weeks. "How did I do that?" is the feeling you have when this synchronicity happens by following your intuitive guidance. If you are not having that feeling, that's a clue that you can practice listening more to your intuition.

Exercises to Strengthen the New Energy of the Intuition Chakra

Use any and all of the following exercises to help you ground the new energy of the intuition chakra into your personal energy system. You can use them as frequently as you find supportive.

Opening Your Third Eye

Massaging your 6th chakra to activate it is a simple exercise to do. Follow these four steps twice a day for a week.

1. Place your middle finger on the point of your 6th chakra.
2. Gently pull your finger up as if you are opening an eyelid, do this 5-6 times.
3. Imagine this third eye opening and blinking and turning on.

A Powerful Prayer to Strengthen Your Intuition

Use the following prayer to ask for reinforcement to sense and follow your intuition: "Dear God, thank you for helping me to know if there is anything I am not supposed to be doing in my life. Please make it increasingly uncomfortable so I am motivated to stop and make a change. Thank you for helping me know and see if there is anything that I should be doing in my life that would be for my highest and greatest good. Make it very obvious to me please, so I cannot miss it."

Handing it to You on a Silver Platter

If you have a habit of doubting yourself and questioning your intuition, or you just don't feel like you get any intuitive hits, ask God or Spirit to give it to you on a silver platter. Just repeat this intention every morning for a week while doing the "Opening Your Third Eye" exercise above: "I am knowing without a shadow of a doubt what is correct and incorrect for me. It's as though it is being handed to me on a silver platter. It is loud and clear and I am confidently moving forward in following through on my intuitive hits."

Connecting Your Intuition and Your Creativity

This exercise will connect the higher-frequency energy of your intuitive chakra to the lower frequency of your creative chakra. Doing this creates an energetic current to allow the higher energies of the 6th chakra to feed the 2nd chakra, which empowers our creation energies to be fed by our insight and intuition.

1. Stand in a comfortable position with your arms and legs uncrossed. Take three deep, relaxing, cleansing breaths.
2. Place the middle finger of one hand on the middle of your stomach, the 2nd or creation chakra. Place the middle finger of your other hand on the middle of your forehead, your intuitive chakra.
3. Imagine you can hook your fingers and pull up, as if you are pulling up a hook gently, lifting the skin in these two locations at the same time.

4. Imagine the 6th chakra talking to the 2nd chakra, as if they are partners, with the 6th chakra supporting the 2nd chakra.

5. Switch your hands at the same time and repeat the hooking process. Keep taking deep, cleansing breaths as you do this.

6. Imagine your chakras are shaking hands, meeting each other saying, "Hello." Your 6th chakra is saying to the 2nd chakra, "I'm here for you to help you raise the frequency of your energy."

7. One more time, switch your hands and do the hook up again. Take a deep cleansing breath.

Mirror Person Exercise to Stop Taking on Other People's Energy

If you are susceptible to taking on other people's energy, you weaken your own chakras. To stop this do the following. When you are around any of these people, be extra mindful of your tendency to take on their energy. You can actually even notice you are about to do it. In your mind, acknowledge that their energy is not your business, nor are you responsible for it. Imagine a wall of mirror surrounding you, reflecting the energy back to the owner and wrapping around them. Imagine a shaft of light coming down through your crown chakra, filling your energy centers, so you have no space to take their energy on. Ask for their healing angels to assist them in working out whatever they need to account for the energy they are creating.

Opening Your Third Eye With Essential Oils

Massage a few drops of essential oils on the location of the 6th chakra on the center of the forehead. Carol Tuttle Healing Oils are custom blends that support you with specific healing goals. These oil blends can be used to activate and strengthen the intuitive chakra in the following ways:

- **I am present:** This oils assists you with opening and activating your intuitive gifts and psychic abilities, which you can use to help yourself and others.
- **I am purpose:** This oil will assist you with aligning your intuitive knowing with your higher purpose. You will receive the inspiration and support of knowing what is the next correct action to take in your life.

What key thing did you learn from this section?

Use this space to make notes. Write down questions and insights you had while reading this section.

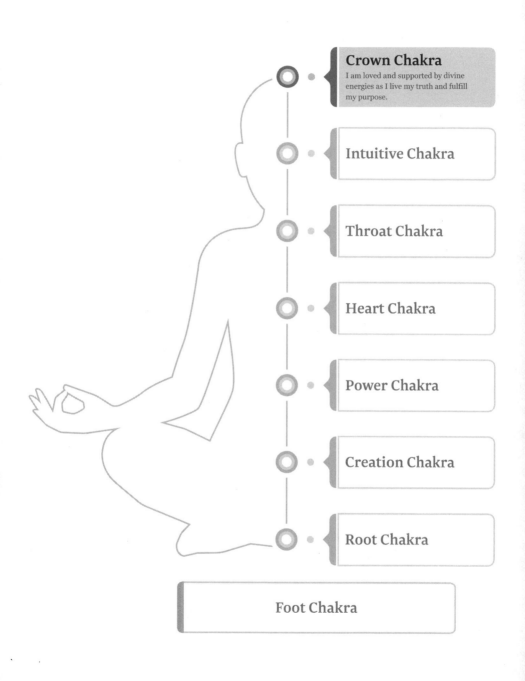

Crown Chakra
I am loved and supported by divine energies as I live my truth and fulfill my purpose.

Intuitive Chakra

Throat Chakra

Heart Chakra

Power Chakra

Creation Chakra

Root Chakra

Foot Chakra

Step 7: Connecting to Your Divine Source

• • • • • • • •

7th Chakra—The Crown Chakra

Location:	Top or crown of the head.
Yin/Yang Flow:	Yin and yang, with the energy first moving into us from heaven, then down through all the chakras below it, connecting us to the earth, then back up again, up through the crown chakra back up to heaven.
Universal Color:	Violet or White
Associated Organs and Body Parts:	Upper brain and hypothalamus. Imbalances in this chakra can manifest physically as headaches, migraines, brain problems, stroke, or other perspective-altering issues.
Function:	Energetically connecting us with our divine source, soul, the higher energies of heaven and the Universe.
Old Energy:	Feeling separated from God and divine energy. Having the illusion that God is punitive and should be feared.
New Energy:	I know I am one with God. Divine strength and power lovingly flow through me at all times.
If Closed:	You feel no connection or guidance from a higher power. You feel unworthy of spiritual help and angry that your higher power has abandoned you. You suffer from migraines and/or tension headaches.
If Open:	You feel connected to divine energy and sense that you are being watched over and cared for. You know you deserve immense blessings. You feel tremendous gratitude for the universal love and appreciation you feel toward yourself and others.
Affirmation:	I am loved and supported by divine energies as I live my truth and fulfill my purpose.
Carol Tuttle Healing Oil Blends:	I am calm I am purpose

The seventh step in awakening brings us into the crown chakra energy. The shift that is occurring in the 7th chakra affects every fiber of our being. This shift is graduating us into the experience of being our own spiritual authority. We let go of feelings of unworthiness easily as we wake up to our truth. Deep down, we know we are worthy, deserving of blessings, watched over and swathed in the love of God. Yet our thinking mind may still run some old patterns and our feelings are learning to catch up with the truth that is awakening in the crown chakra.

THE OLD ENERGY OF THE CROWN CHAKRA

For centuries, the old energy of the crown chakra has played out two particular themes in our experience with God and divinity. The first is feeling separate and even abandoned by God and the second is believing that God is punitive and is to be feared. We have been awakening from these lies and illusions for decades now.

FEELING SEPARATE FROM GOD

Feeling separated from God is a common feeling that can affect many areas of our lives. We may not even be consciously aware of it. One of the most powerful clearing sessions that I offer in the Carol Tuttle Healing Center is titled, *Clearing Session for Pre-Birth Trauma*. In this clearing, you clear deeply held beliefs to free yourself from the illusion that you are separated from God. Here is part of the transcript from that clearing session:

> *This clearing will help you release any energy you may still carry that could have been caused by any perceptions you may have developed prior to coming to the Earth that you are being separated from God.*

Take a deep breath and let go of the following deeper beliefs by repeating these phrases out loud:

Letting go of unsafe, afraid, anxious, nervous.

Sad to leave the light. Sad to leave God. I won't make it.

Afraid I can't do this. Risk that I may never get back.

Releasing from all levels and layers of my being not ready to leave.

Wanting to hide, wanting to stop the process, resentful.

I don't like my family.

Too much dysfunction.

Losing myself in the family story.

Angry that I chose this family. What was I thinking?

Release all the trapped trauma energy including regret, disillusioned, feeling separate, pessimistic.

Nobody prepared me for this. Wanting to change my mind, can't. Let it all go."

Where am I? Who am I? Losing myself, feeling disconnected from my true self.

Wishing I hadn't done this. Releasing all of the times I have felt lost, confused, in limbo. Can't move forward, can't move back.

Where am I? Who am I?

Regret. Made a mistake. Don't trust myself. Let it all go.

Releasing all of the energy of feeling small, insignificant, unwanted, illegitimate.

Take a deep, cleansing breath and as you exhale, let all of the above illusions go.

To fill the space you have just cleared with truths, repeat the following phrases out loud:

I am ready. I am confident in my choices. I make wise decisions.
I am staying connected to my true self and to the divine.
I'm making a difference in my family. I'm wanted. I am desired.
I am moving forward with confidence. I am successful.
I am remembering who I am. I am confident. I am ready.
I am present. I am protected. I am at peace. I am calm.

Take a deep breath. Close your eyes and let it sink in. Come back
and repeat this clearing and reframing exercise anytime you
feel alone, separate, unsupported and abandoned by God. This
powerful clearing will support you in feeling connected to God
and support you in building self-confidence and holding your own
energy so you can create success and affluence in all areas of your
life.

PUNITIVE GOD VS. BENEVOLENT GOD

We are shifting out of the hellfire and brimstone era of how humanity has perceived God. We are more and more aware that shame, guilt, and fear are not healthy motivators to do what we feel is correct and right and to choose and teach obedience. However, there are still remnants of this old perception in most religious experiences in the way things are phrased and sometimes taught.

When I was actively raising my family and we would attend church on Sunday, it was not uncommon when we came home that I would debrief my kids and tell them that God is a god of love and honor and that we just needed to ignore the words that some people choose to use. That is just how some people were taught in respect to their relationship and understanding of God.

In 2010, a religious poll of 1,426 Americans showed that "people who believe in an angry, vengeful god are more likely to suffer from social anxiety, paranoia, obsessional thinking, and compulsions. Poll respondents who indicated belief in a deity were placed in three categories: those who believed in a punitive god, those who believed in a benevolent god, and those who believed in a deistic (uninvolved) god. Then the researchers looked at the prevalence of emotional problems in each group. What exactly did the researchers find? Symptoms of mental illness were more common among those in the punitive god group than in the deistic god or benevolent god groups." The belief in a punitive god is consistent with the old energy of this chakra and continuing to hold onto it creates discomfort.

My daughter Anne shares how she perceives and experiences who God is:

"I have always viewed God as my loving Heavenly Father that cares deeply for me. He is kind and compassionate. He is a God of abundant love and showers me with all my blessings. He guides my learning in life. I feel a strong connection to Him and I am grateful for the purpose I find in life knowing that I am a child of God."

My youngest son Mark has put a lot of thought in to who God is and his relationship with God. He shares his experience in the following:

"I have never really thought of God wanting to punish me, it just doesn't correspond with everything I have learned, and experienced in my relationship with God. Even though I recognize God as my supreme creator and the source of all the good I

experience, I believe that it is up to me to claim those blessings and create a joyful life.

I know from experience that the closer I follow inspired actions and allow love to guide my actions then as a result I will have a happier and more joy-filled life. I know that I am more care-free, and free to use my power for myself to create a wonderful and happy life when I live according to my faith-based principles.

To live in fear of the "wrath" of God or to believe that God is "vengeful" never played a role in my relationship with Him. Again, it comes back to what we want to create; what we focus on doesn't play sides, so if we focus on fear and scarcity, then we will create those experiences. Likewise, when we are actively seeking hope and abundance then we will experience that."

A member of the Healing Center shared the following in her experience in re-creating her connection with divinity from a negative perception of God to a positive one:

"I am so grateful for Carol and the tools she has provided for us! I have been struggling with self-worth for most of my life. I was given up for adoption as an infant. I was raised in a very strict Catholic household, and while it wasn't explicitly stated, the idea of unworthiness was everywhere. In fact, my "favorite" hymn was called "Oh Lord, I am Not Worthy"! I sometimes struggle with using the word "God" in these clearings because the God I was raised with thought I was an awful sinner and was most likely going to hell. I am so grateful for the clearings that are helping me

move to a new life of affluence, ease, and joy and to understand that I am special to God."

THE NEW ENERGY OF THE CROWN CHAKRA

The new energy of the crown chakra is meant to connect us to the divine in a way that inspires us, rather than shames us. There is no intellectual knowing at the level of 7th chakra, but there is serenity, joy, and deep peace about life. You have a sense of knowing that there is a deeper meaning of life and that there is an order that underlies all of existence so you easily let things go as you are not attached to the outcomes.

We connect with our soul understanding about our life path and are able to feel tremendous gratitude for all that we have experienced and all of the people who have played parts for us. When we realize that everything is interconnected, that we are part of the larger scheme of life, and that everything that happened in our life happened for a reason, we begin to live with gratitude, faith, and trust, rather than filled with fear and anxiety.

The following are indicators that the new energy of the 7th chakra is getting activated for you and you are feeling more and more connection with divine energies. How many of these have you experienced?

- You are experiencing spirituality as an internal and personal experience that can be supported by outside influences of your choosing.
- You are changing your perception of God and deity to be more positive.
- You are waking up to the truth that you are the creator of your life and you can create more affluence, ease, and joy.

- You are deeply moved to heal any interferences that keep you stifled and compromised from living your true self.
- You are letting go of judgments of others. You notice when you are complaining or judging and you do not like how it makes you feel.
- Even though the world can be energetically chaotic and turbulent, you are sensing a growing state of peace and well-being inside of you.
- You feel connected to God, the universe, your soul, and other spiritual support systems that are there for you.

The new energy of the crown chakra is waking us up to the truth that we are guided by higher powers as we are feeling and sensing divinity from within and without. The energy that comes down into our personal energy system feeds the entire chakra system, feeding us a new energy to help us create a new reality.

BECOMING THE OBSERVER AND THE OBSERVED

When you are operating from your crown chakra, you are in the highest state of awareness that you can be in. You have moments in your life when you feel you are observing your own experience from a place of higher consciousness. You feel you are separate, yet one with the event that is playing out. From the position of observer, you can actually will or intend the experience to shift in a more favorable direction and support yourself in creating a positive outcome of any situation. You are not emotionally drawn into the story that is unfolding and you are able to stay composed as if you are watching yourself in a movie.

I remember the first time I had a 7th chakra experience. I was just 21 years old. I had been dating a young man who I was convinced I would marry. Having not yet healed my father wounds and the lack of emotional connection from a healthy bond with him, I was vulnerable to being very needy. I played out that neediness with this young man by becoming emotionally attached to him. He led me to believe for several months that the feelings were mutual. Then one day, out of the blue, he stopped calling me and seeing me. No explanation, he just disappeared. I was devastated and in hindsight, I now realize his decision to stop any contact with me had triggered very deep feelings of abandonment that were really about my dad. Yet I did not have the awareness to know that yet. I just knew I hurt more emotionally than I had ever hurt in my life. I was devastated to a point that it was difficult functioning day to day. I remember praying and pleading for relief and healing of the emotional overwhelm I was in. Several weeks after his disappearance, I ran into this young man on our college campus. During our brief exchange, I felt as if the top of my head opened and all of the energy that was emotionally weighing me down was lifted from me. I was overcome with a feeling of well-being and peace. I felt a wholeness inside of me that was new to me as I felt the Spirit fill my being. I left that young man's presence as a different person, having reclaimed a part of me and becoming more aware and awake then I had ever been at that time in my life. As I walked away, I silently thanked him and wished him well. I was free. I never felt the emotional longing for him that I thought was about him. It wasn't. It was about the feeling of unmet needs from a father who had never bonded with me. God blessed me that day. Years later, as I studied the chakra system, I realized which part of my energy system had played all this out. I can still recall how I felt that afternoon when I was in college because it had a life-changing effect on me.

For the first time in my life I felt the powerful function of the the 7th chakra's yin and yang energy, as a receiver and giver of energy and consciousness. The crown chakra receives energy to sustain us and feed our personal energy system and it gives back the personal energy into the energetic network of humanity to unite the collective pool of consciousness.

The challenge of this chakra is to not get pulled out too far into higher states of consciousness to the point that we are not grounded or we don't want to be. As we are liberated by the spirit and are opened to divine energies we need to stay firmly rooted to our bodies and the physical world. The awakening of the 7th chakra is connecting us to our source of enlightenment, to our higher selves, to every being on the planet, and ultimately the divine energy that creates everything in the universe. As we embody these new energies, we bless the lives of everyone we meet just by being in the space.

My husband had a unique and powerful life-changing event that literally blew open his crown chakra. At the young age of 55, he experienced a full-on stroke. At about 5:15 pm on a Friday afternoon, we were finishing up work at our offices. Present at the office were myself, Jon, and our daughter Anne who was full-term with her first baby. She had hung around to finish up her work. Jon was standing in the doorway of my office chatting with me when suddenly, his speech started to slur. I thought he was just messing around with me until I saw him grab the left side of his body and then drop to the ground, crying. He knew that something frightening was going on and could not talk to tell me what was happening. I ran to my daughter who quickly called 911. In less than 10 minutes the "Men of Thor" (as I call EMTs and firemen) showed up. Not much later, I was in the back of an ambulance, speeding down the highway with my husband.

Jon was officially diagnosed as having a stroke and received the TPA drug that suspends the side effects of a stroke. The most significant damage Jon incurred to his brain affected his ability to speak. He could not speak. His thoughts were clear and he knew what he wanted to say, but could not produce the words. As is common for stroke victims with this kind of brain damage, they get stuck on only one word that comes out when they attempt to speak. Jon's word was "grey." Jon was in the intensive care unit for five days and then moved to a physical therapy unit for ten days. He then followed up with 3-4 months of intensive speech therapy. Jon worked hard and fully and completely recovered. You would never know today that he had a stroke. He is healthy and vital and fully able to speak. The one thing the stroke did change for Jon was his spiritual experience with himself and his connection to God. In my words, Jon's crown chakra was blown open. In Jon's words he shares:

"I thought I was in pretty good physical shape prior to my stroke. The 10 years prior I had ran 14 marathons and was just finishing up my 16th Sprint Triathlon. As Carol has shared, the stroke occurred with no signs of it coming on. I was at our offices working late with Carol and my daughter Anne. I had a headache that day that wouldn't go away, but did not think it was anything out of the ordinary. I was just about to leave to play tennis when my speech started slurring and my body went numb and I fell to the floor. Carol screamed and Anne went into action calling 911.

I didn't know what was happening to me and I was terrified. As a result of the stroke and the damage that my brain had incurred, I couldn't talk, or write, and I had trouble remembering names and how to read.

Thankfully, I have had a full and complete recovery. Physically you wouldn't be able to tell that I had a major stroke. I have slight aphasia where I can't always say the words that I intend to say. I have some trouble focusing on reading for a long time, and have slight numbness in my right toes. I always say that I was certainly blessed and very lucky.

What changed for me was more mental and spiritual. The best way to say it is to mention that before my stroke, I was quite judgmental of people's actions, thinking that their choices were good or bad, based on my belief system. However, after my stroke, I no longer saw people's choices and life experiences in such a strict reference to being right or wrong or good and evil. I was raised in a strict religious family that had strongly influenced my view of people and the world in a much more defined reference of there is good and evil in the world and you are either choosing good or you are choosing evil. I had been taught that we had to please God and obey what was right or we would be unfavorable in God's eyes.

It was an incredible and different experience post-stroke to now experience people's choices as simply choices—choices that created a cause and effect of outcomes that would transpire in their lives. That there were choices that brought positive effects into our lives and choices that caused negative effects in our lives, but the choices did not define whether we were good or evil in God's perception of us.

I no longer hold an image of a Supreme Being judging me for my choices that I will either please or dis-please. I now connect with

God on a much deeper level as a being of great patience, kindness, and incredibly loving and only able to see the truth of who I am. Anything less than that is my perception.

Several years after my stroke, I had a SPECT scan performed on my brain. The psychiatrist that I met with to go over the results of my brain scan shared with me and Carol, that the area of my brain that holds the understanding of God within a learned religious construct (the area called the precuneus in the parietal lobe) had been damaged. Along with losing my ability to speak, I had also lost all the learning of what I had been taught as a child about who God is and how to interpret my religious teachings based on perceptions and understandings my parents had taught.

For a long time, I felt like a fish out of water, practicing the religion of my childhood. I did not know how to worship and participate without the old references anymore. It was a difficult time having my familiar belief system taken away. I went through many months of guilt and questioning how to move forward without the old references of God.

I later came to know that this has been a blessing for me. It has allowed me to open to the great love God has for us and to no longer view the world and the people of the world through a judgmental lens. I participate in my religious faith from a different perspective that is more aligned with a perspective that Carol has been growing in for years—that God loves us, that we are always worthy, and it is up to us to determine the quality of life we want, based on the cause and effect of our choices. If we want a blessed life, we make choices that allow that, if we want struggle and pain, we make choices that provoke that. I trust God and know that as I follow my own authority and what is correct for me, I will be led and guided by the inner promptings I am given, rather than having to look outside myself from a place of fear to make sure I do what is right."

As an observer, I have noticed that wherever I go with my husband in public, a large group of people ALWAYS come into the space after him. We can be the only two people at a restaurant and within five minutes 20 people will walk in. We recently took our grandsons to an ice cream shop and we weren't too impressed with the ice cream. I made a comment about whether or not they would stay in business, as we were the only ones there. By the time we had finished our ice cream, three families or about 15 people had come into the shop. I've told Jon many times, "Businesses should hire you to just stand in their space, because a crowd always shows up wherever you are!" This phenomenon only started happening after Jon had his stroke.

Could it be that my husband has such an open crown chakra now with a beautiful white light streaming through it that he attracts crowds wherever he goes? People are yearning for more light and truth in a world that seems dark and murky in the bigger scheme of things. As you work on activating your crown chakra to allow the new energies of light to come into you, you also will be like a magnet for others to seek you out. Others will want to be in your space to feel the divine love that is the origin of our beginnings. Continue to open yourself to the divine energy that is there for you first and then for others, to bless their lives.

HOW TO ATTAIN A CONNECTION TO
THESE HIGHER ENERGIES

After reading about the new energy of the 7th chakra, you may think that it seems out of reach for you. You may think, "Well, that sounds nice for monks and gurus, but not for me. I'm just an ordinary person with a normal life."

While we do have the demands of daily living and the busy minds that accompany these demands, staying connected to our higher selves and divine energies may not be as far off as it appears. A worthy goal may be to live in a constant state of pure awareness. But how about living with moments of pure awareness? We have all experienced these moments at one time or another. Have you ever felt unconditional love for someone? Have you ever experienced a miracle?

Practicing meditation, prayer, and daily silence are disciplines that lead to increased moments of spiritual connection. Every time you stop what you are doing and just notice your breathing, you are calling yourself into present moment awareness, and when you are in present moment awareness you are connecting to higher energies. In fact, try it right now. Close your eyes and just notice your breathing. How many breaths were you able to stay aware of before your mind was pulled out to your next thought? Modern-day technology can support you in activating your modern-day chakras. For example, I use the *Breethe* app (which is available for free) to remind me to take moments each day just for breathing. The *Calm* app prompts you every day to go into states of relaxation and calm which help you connect with these higher energies.

Once you've established a daily practice of these activities that connect you to universal consciousness, you will see expansion of spiritual awareness in your outer world. You will begin to experience unconditional love on a consistent basis. You will be more compassionate, kind, and forgiving, and you will show more humility. Life will no longer be solely about you and your desires. Your life will become more about serving others because when you serve others, you are serving yourself.

Exercises to Strengthen the New Energy of the Crown Chakra

Use any and all of the following exercises to help you ground the new energy of the crown chakra into your personal energy system. You can use them as frequently as you find supportive.

Breathing Techniques

Alternate nostril breathing is done by covering one nostril as you inhale. At the top of the inhale, momentarily hold your breath. Switch to the other nostril and cover it as you exhale. Then take another inhale. At the top of that inhale, momentarily hold your breath, cover the other nostril and exhale followed by your next inhale. Keep repeating this cycle for 3-5 minutes.

Doing Yoga

Any pose that brings the head to the floor, like downward dog, fish pose, or happy baby pose will support connection and activation of your crown chakra. Right after you get out of bed, do each of these poses.

Meditating

Using a meditation app like Headspace or Calm, start practicing meditation every day starting with five minutes and increasing it to at least ten.

Actively Meditating with Tibetan Singing Bowls

I own nine different Tibetan singing bowls and use them on a regular basis. I find it is more supportive for me to meditate and quiet my mind and body while I am playing my bowls along with deep breathing exercises.

Of all the bowls I own, seven of them are chakra bowls. The notes and frequencies that the bowls each play help open up each of the seven chakras they coordinate with. I have recorded custom sound tracks of different Tibetan singing bowl meditations that are available in my online Healing Center. You can also find some remarkable and supportive soundtracks of Tibetan singing bowls on YouTube.

Doing the Crown Pull

Use this exercise any time your mind is overactive and you want to open yourself to intuition and spiritual guidance and spiritual guidance. I learned this technique from my mentor, Donna Eden:

1. Stand up and take three deep, cleansing breaths.
2. Put your fingertips in the middle of your forehead, on your 6th chakra.
3. Pull your fingertips apart toward your temples. Bring your fingertips together again, just above the place you started on your forehead.
4. Pull your fingertips apart again. Continue to do this all the way up and around the crown of the head until you get to the back of the neck.
5. Hang your hands off your neck with your elbows falling in your front your face.
6. Take three deep, cleansing breaths.

Opening Your Crown Chakra With Essential Oils

Massage a few drops of essential oils on the location of the 7th chakra on the crown of the head. Carol Tuttle Healing Oils are custom blends that support you with specific healing goals. These oil blends can be used to activate and strengthen the crown chakra in the following ways:

- **I am calm:** This oil will assist you in connecting with your higher states of awareness and pull you back into a place of calmness by activating the right brain hemisphere and the pineal gland. As you place the oil on the crown of the head and hold your hand on top of your head for several minutes, you will come back into your body, into present-moment awareness, with the sense that everything is going to be okay.
- **I am purpose:** This oil will assist you in connecting your crown chakra with the energy of God and your highest self. As your crown chakra strengthens, you will have a live stream of divine energy supporting you every day of your life.

What key thing did you learn from this section?

Use this space to make notes. Write down questions and insights you had while reading this section.

Final Thoughts as You Finish the 7 Steps to Awakening

• • • • • • •

I am happy and excited for you. You have now walked through the seven steps of your chakra energy. As you have read this book, you have connected with and activated each of your chakras. Your desire and intention to improve the quality of your life through your study and practice of the chakras will take you into the next level of well-being and joy.

As you continue to study and apply the principles and exercises you've learned in this book, I promise you that your life will only get better and more full of abundant living.

Walking through these seven steps of awakening by reading this book is not a one-time experience. It is a lifestyle. Your chakra energy is working for you and talking to you every day. Take time every day to fine-tune your chakra energy. Return to this book often to continue to learn and expand. As a result, you are sure to experience a richer and more vibrant life. Expect your health to improve, your relationships to blossom, and your finances to soar.

I am here for you, so please reach out to my support team if we can do anything for you. Congratulations! You are a remarkable person.

With love
Carol Tuttle
carol@caroltuttle.com

Resources From Carol Tuttle
To Support Your Healing

• • • • • • •

Books by Carol Tuttle

Mastering Affluence

Remembering Wholeness

It's Just My Nature

The Child Whisperer

Online resources by Carol Tuttle

CarolTuttle.com

HealWithCarol.com

MyEnergyProfile.com

The30DayMoneyCure.com

DressingYourTruth.com

DYTMen.com

TheChildWhisperer.com

Online Courses by Carol Tuttle

The Carol Tuttle Healing Center

Energy Profiling

The 30-Day Money Cure

Dressing Your Truth for Women

Dressing Your Truth for Men

Go deeper and learn more about your personal chakra energy system in The Carol Tuttle Healing Center. Along with an extensive library of 100+ online healing sessions and guided healing plans, there are numerous chakra healing resources. Sign up for your free trial at healwithcarol.com

For more information on my Energy Profiling system mentioned in this book, go to myenergyprofile.com and learn your Type for free.

Endnotes

· · · · · · ·

1. Margery Williams, *The Velveteen Rabbit*, (New York: Holt, Rinehart and Winston, 1983).

2. Caroline Myss, *Anatomy of the Spirit: The Seven Stages of Power and Healing*, (New York: Harmony Books, 1996).

3. Timothy Burgin, "The Vedas," *Yoga Basics*, March 2016, https://www.yogabasics.com/learn/the-vedas/

4. "*Encyclopaedia Britannica*, s.v. "Chakra," Chicago: Encyclopaedia Britannica, 2009. https://www.britannica.com/topic/chakra (accessed July 2019).

5. Sir John Woodroffe, The Serpent Power, (Madras, India: Ganesh & Co., reprint 2003).

6. Anodea Judith, *Wheels of Life: A User's Guide to the Chakra System*, (Woodbury, MN: Llewellyn Publications, 1987).

7. Caroline Myss, *Anatomy of the Spirit: The Seven Stages of Power and Healing*, (New York: Harmony Books, 1996).

8. Carol Tuttle, *Mastering Affluence*, (Salt Lake City: Live Your Truth Press, 2018).

9. Robert M. Sargis, MD, PhD, "An Overview of the Pineal Gland," Endocrine Web, https://www.endocrineweb.com/endocrinology/overview-pineal-gland

10. Hiroshi Motoyama, *Theories of the Chakras: Bridge to Higher Consciousness*, (Wheaton: Theosophical Publishing House, 1982).

11. Dr Valerie Hunt, *Infinite Mind: Science of Human Vibrations of Consciousness*, 2nd ed. (Malibu Pub, 1996).

12. Leonard A. Wisneski and Lucy Anderson, *The Scientific Basis of Integrative Medicine*, (Boca Raton: CRC Press, 2009).

13. Pradeep B. Deshpande, P. Krishna Madappa, and Konstantin Korotkov, "Can the Excellence of the Internal Be Measured?" *The Journal of Consciousness Exploration and Research*, 4, no. 9, (Nov 2013): 977-987, https://cdn3.collective-evolution.com/assets/uploads/2014/03/Can-Internal-Excellence-be-Measured_Deshpande.pdf

14. "The Sacred Hawaiian Islands," My Mahana. https://www.mymahana.com/blogs/news/34907588-the-sacred-hawaiian-islands

15. Ken Rubin, "The Formation of the Hawaiian Islands," Hawaii Center for Volcanology, https://www.soest.hawaii.edu/GG/HCV/haw_formation.html

16. Maui Whale Season, Maui Whale Watching Official Guide, https://mauiwhalewatching.com/

17. Madeline Stone, "9 Crazy Facts About Larry Ellison's Hawaiian Island," *Business Insider*, September 2014, https://www.businessinsider.com/9-crazy-facts-about-lanai-2014-9

18. "The Island of Molokai," Hawaii.com, https://www.hawaii.com/molokai/

19. "Oahu: The Gathering Place," Beyond Honolulu, https://beyondhonolulu.com/oahu-the-gathering-place/

20. "Today in History – Dec 1, Rosa Parks Arrested," Library of Congress. https://www.loc.gov/item/today-in-history/december-01/

21. Haley Sweetland Edwards, "How Christine Blasey Ford's Testimony Changed America," *TIME*, https://time.com/5415027/christine-blasey-ford-testimony/

22. Malala Yousafzai, "Malala's Story," The Malala Fund, https://www.malala.org/malalas-story

23. Carol Tuttle, *Mastering Affluence*, (Salt Lake City: Live Your Truth Press, 2018).

24. Sheri Winston, *Women's Anatomy of Arousal*, (New York: Mango Garden Press, 2010).

25. Dr. Christiane Northrup, *Women's Bodies, Women's Wisdom*, (New York: Bantam Dell, 1994).

26. Ellen Bass and Laura Davis, *The Courage to Heal: A Guide for Women Survivors of Child Sexual Abuse*, (New York: Harper & Row, 1988).

27. The 5th Dimension, "Age of Aquarius/Let the Sun Shine In," *Hair*, Soul City, 1969

28. "Why is the vernal equinox called the 'First Point of Aries' when the Sun is actually in Pisces on this date?" University of Southern Maine. https://usm.maine.edu/planet/why-vernal-equinox-called-first-point-aries-when-sun-actually-pisces-date

29. Portia Nelson, "Autobiography in Five Short Chapters," *There's a Hole in My Sidewalk: The Romance of Self-Discovery*, (Beyond Words Publishing, reprint 1993).

30. Laura Schocker, "Marie Kondo Says Her Parents Once Banned Her From Tidying," Apartment Therapy, https://www.apartmenttherapy.com/marie-kondo-tidying-childhood-home-266273

31. Dr. Susan Forward with Craig Buck, *Toxic Parents: Overcoming Their Hurtful Legacy and Reclaiming Your Life*, (New York: Bantam, 1989), 187-189.

32. Will Bowen, *A Complaint Free World: How to Stop Complaining and Start Enjoying the Life You Always Wanted*, (New York: Three Rivers Press, 2007).

33. Bernard Marr, "How Much Data Do We Create Every Day? The Mind-Blowing Stats Everyone Should Read," *Forbes*, May 21, 2018, https://www.forbes.com/sites/bernardmarr/2018/05/21/how-much-data-do-we-create-every-day-the-mind-blowing-stats-everyone-should-read/

34. Carol Tuttle, "Everyone is Psychic," *Remembering Wholeness*, (Seattle: Sea Script Company, 2000).

35. Headspace. https://www.headspace.com/

36. Dr. Sarah Schewitz, PsyD, "11 Women On How They Know Their Intuition Is Speaking to Them," Bustle, https://www.bustle.com/p/11-women-on-how-they-know-their-intuition-is-speaking-to-them-13262052